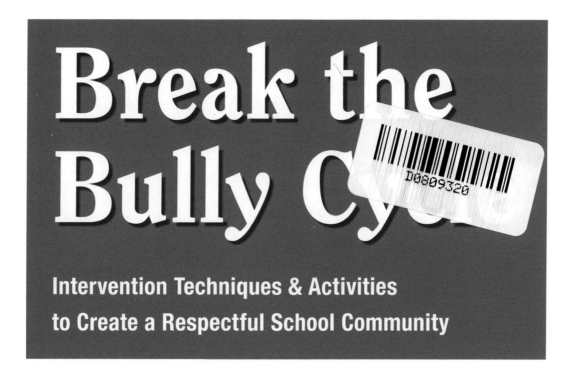

Break the Bully Cycle

Intervention Techniques & Activities to Create a Respectful School Community

SiriNam S. Khalsa, NBCT

A GOOD YEAR BOOK™

Good Year Books
Tucson, Arizona

Dedication

This book is sincerely dedicated to my wife, Kirn Kaur, for her perseverance through life's adversities and dedication to being a caring mother and loving wife, and to my children, Ananda, Dharam Bir, and Karta, who freely share their insights and school experiences.

Good Year Books

Our titles are available for most basic curriculum subjects plus many enrichment areas. For information on other Good Year Books and to place orders, contact your local bookseller or educational dealer, or visit our website at www.goodyearbooks.com. For a complete catalog, please contact:

Good Year Books
PO Box 91858
Tucson, AZ 85752-1858
www.goodyearbooks.com

Cover Design: Gary Smith, Performance Design
Text Design: Doug Goewey
Drawings: Nathan Schiel

ISBN-10: 1-59647-119-0
ISBN-13: 978-1-59647-119-1
ISBN-eBook: 978-1-59647-215-0

1 2 3 4 5 6 7 8 9   12 11 10 09 08 07

About the Author

SiriNam S. Khalsa, M.S. Ed., is a National Board Certified Teacher, Inclusion Coach, seminar leader, and author. In addition to his work as an Inclusion Coach for educators teaching in mixed-ability classrooms in the Springfield, Massachusetts, schools, he is also a Professional Development Associate for the Massachusetts Teacher Association (MTA). Khalsa has received special recognition from the governor of Massachusetts, and in 1993 he was honored as Special Education Teacher of the Year in that state. He has been awarded the title Distinguished Teacher to honor his excellence in teaching and was a 2004 Massachusetts Teacher of the Year finalist. In addition to this book, he has authored *Inclusive Classroom* (Good Year Books, 2005), *Teaching Discipline and Self-respect* (Corwin Press, 2007), *Differentiated Instruction* (TEACHINGpoint 2004), and *Group Exercises for Enhancing Social Skills and Self-Esteem 1&2* (Professional Resource Press, 1996 & 1998).

If you are interested in sponsoring a dynamic workshop in your school district, please contact:

SiriNam S. Khalsa
131 Montague Road
Leverett, MA 01054
413-575-2533
sirinam1@rcn.com

Acknowledgments

I want to recognize my colleagues and friends who have dedicated their time and energy toward keeping our schools safe and nurturing for all students. I appreciate their commitment to this mission and the ideas they have shared with me for promoting safe schools and positive peer relationships.

I also want to thank Good Year Books for believing in this book, and especially Bobbie Dempsey, for her help and encouragement during writing, editing, and production. And last but not least, I thank you for picking up this book and showing your interest in making your school an environment that is safe and free from the problems bullying can bring.

Contents

Contents

Introduction

O ne of the major problems facing children and teenagers today in our schools is bullying. Most students have to deal with a bullying problem at some point in their lives. Consider these statistics:

◇ Schools across the United States harbor approximately 5 million bullies and 5.5 million of their victims (D. Owens, National School Safety Center). According to the National Association of School Psychologists (NASP), one in seven school children is a bully or a victim.

◇ Sixty-five percent of students in schools have reported being bullied. Twelve percent were bullied on a regular basis and 13 percent bullied other students once or more a week (Center for Youth Development).

◇ Recent studies by CBS News show that an alarming number of teenagers, usually boys but sometimes girls, are driven to suicide by schoolyard bullying. Suicides may be the exception to everyday life in most schools, where bullying is less dramatic but still common.

We know that bullying begins in preschool and seems to reach its peak during the middle school years. Bullying behavior in elementary school can easily turn into violence by middle school and high school. Jack, who is a bully at age eight, is *three times more likely* to be convicted of a crime by age thirty and less likely to find a meaningful profession. Cindy, who is a thirteen-year-old bully, is more likely to raise children who become bullies. We hear and read about abusive spouses and workplace bullying because studies show that childhood bullying grows into workplace bullying and that children who are victims of bullies often become victims as adults. This underscores the fact that bullying is a learned behavior, and a bully will not change by simply growing up. To avoid becoming adult bullies and victims, young bullies must be taught better ways of relating to others and young victims must be given the skills to be more assertive in their interpersonal relationships.

> **Key Concept**
>
> *Experience tells us that the abundance of a problem does not bring about change until direct intervention and direct action takes place.*

Teachers, parents, students, and others are creating a growing number of anti-bullying programs. However, despite the serious social problem we have in our schools with bullies and victims, the issue has been largely overlooked. Children can be naturally self-centered and may make hurtful remarks during a conflict, but a quarrel or one-time fight is not bullying. *Bullying occurs when a child is the target of repeated negative actions by someone else, usually a peer.* Not unlike sexual harassment, bullying is so widespread and so common that the integration of so-called "normal growing-up behavior" has blinded us to its extensive harm.

We do know that teachers and parents can have a profound effect on a child's behavior and the school climate. To begin the process of change, it's equally important to know what you *don't know* about bullies and victims.

Bully Facts:

- Bullying is a learned behavior.

- Boys and girls both bully, but their tactics are usually different.

- Bullies tend to be average students academically.

- Bullies come in all sizes. Sometimes they may intimidate victims who are larger than they are if there is an imbalance of power due to age or peer support.

- Bullies have an inflated self-concept but usually have low self-esteem or feel inferior to others, which reflects a strong need to dominate with threats.

- Bullies lack empathy for their victims and feel justified in their actions.

- Reciprocal aggression doesn't usually stop the victim from being bullied. In fact it may incite the bully to future attacks. Assertive versus aggressive behavior is most effective.

- When dealing with a bullying incident, it is usually more effective to meet with parents apart from meeting with bullies and victims. Parents are emotionally involved, so a meeting will be beneficial.

What Can Be Done?

Break the Bully Cycle provides teachers, parents, and all school personnel with insight into this problem and specific interventions that address the needs of the school and community. This book is not a program. Rather, it's specific information to educate the user, along with a collection of interventions, strategies, and activities designed to address the multifaceted problem of bullying in today's schools. If your school presently has an anti-bullying program in place, you might find this book a useful supplement to the existing program. If it doesn't have a defined anti-bullying program, then use this book to help start one. The goal is to take purposeful action to meet the unique needs of your classroom and school.

The Wimpy Caterpillar

One of my colleagues, Ms. Cook, recently shared a conversation with me that she had had with one of her students. This student had recently graduated from college and was looking for work. Her student, George, was a bully in middle school and almost got expelled for hurting another student. George reminded Ms. Cook of a conversation they had had one day after school that seemed to be a turning point in his aggression toward others. Ms. Cook explained to George that he reminded her of one of those fuzzy caterpillars that have long extended tentacles and look pretty scary, but when you touch them they roll into a small, tight ball. George remembered Ms. Cook asking him why he thought the caterpillar looked so scary. He responded, "To keep his enemies away." She then asked him what he thought the caterpillar was really feeling, especially after being touched by someone else. George wasn't sure so Ms. Cook said, "The caterpillar is actually scared of other creatures and is feeling kind of wimpy inside." Then she told him that she thought that was how George felt when he teased and picked on other kids. In order to feel powerful and big, he needed to harass someone else. George remembered Ms. Cook then asking him if he wanted to keep this conversation between themselves or discuss it with other kids in his class. He opted to keep it between themselves. George and Ms. Cook had several subsequent conversations as he gradually related to her as his mentor teacher. Fortunately, George began rethinking how he related to others, and in high school he took out his aggression playing football and being part of the wrestling team.

We should never underestimate our ability to make a difference in a child's life. Ms. Cook happened to tell the right story at the right time in this student's life. Unfortunately, few bullies change so quickly or have the insight that George possessed but as teachers and parents, we are shaping young lives. When children are in elementary and middle school, their minds are like Jello. We need to put a lot of good thoughts into their minds before they set. By reaching out to your students, and treating them with respect and dignity, you're giving them what all students need: positive role modeling and caring from a healthy adult. In general that is what this book is teaching: how to effectively interact with all students by showing them by example what behaviors you expect from them and then providing opportunities for them to change their bullying and victim habits. By doing this, we are empowering children to prevent and solve their problems.

This book is divided into six chapters. Chapter 1 provides an overview of bullying. Chapter 2 addresses the foundation of change, which is creating a cooperative classroom environment. It also includes techniques and activities designed to heighten awareness of the bully and victim problem as well as to change everyone's attitudes and behaviors for the better. Chapters 3 and 4 discuss victims and bullies, respectively, and how you can help both. Chapter 5 provides information and interventions on how to keep a safe and secure school community. One of the most effective deterrents to bullying and aggression in school is adult intervention with student support. This chapter provides strategies for working with potentially violent students and offers activities that can help create safer schools *and* school buses. The final chapter addresses the rising problem of cyberbullying.

The dual purpose of this book, intervention and prevention, alerts adults and children to the difference between "normal teasing" and bullying situations. Once you understand these dynamics, this book will help you act effectively when children are bullying or being bullied. Stopping a bullying situation is not enough unless we can also cultivate a school climate that prevents the attitudes and behaviors that may have caused the problem to arise. Aggressive behavior is an innate human response more prevalent with young minds and underdeveloped egos. We cannot expect to eliminate all aggressive acts in today's schools, but we can put limits on it where children's interactions and well-being are concerned. This book is written to educate, empower and encourage children and adults, students and teachers, to work in partnership to prevent bullying in our schools across the country. If you do have a bullying problem, regardless of how large or small, you'll be taking concrete steps to improve the lives of your students. If you do not take steps to address the problem, cruelty will continue to grow and be overlooked and, therefore, be condoned, and children will suffer.

I hope this book can help you, your classroom, and your school community become a place where all students are free to work and learn without the fear of being harassed. You as the teacher, counselor, or administrator also have the right to teach without the ongoing concern about bullies and victims, and parents have the right to feel their children are being looked after. Let us know at Good Year Books how these interventions are working. I welcome your questions, comments, and suggestions.

—SiriNam S. Khalsa

Chapter 1

Bullying: An Overview

"Out of sight, out of mind."

What Is Bullying?

Bullying takes place when one or more individuals use threats of bodily harm, assault, or battery to cause physical, verbal, or emotional harm to another individual. Simply stated, bullying is any behavior that is hurtful to someone else's physical, emotional, or mental self, regardless if the person intended it to be hurtful or not. It is not something to be minimized. Bullies attempt to control their peers by using verbal or physical threats that can turn into assaults. They choose their victims carefully, finding those who are unpopular and vulnerable to aggressive acts.

People are not born bullies. They often become bullies after being bullied when they were young. It is a learned behavior that has taken on a persona that enables a child to feel psychologically big and powerful. Research points out that by age thirty, approximately 25 percent of adults who were bullies as children have a criminal record. This demonstrates the urgency of early intervention.

Teasing and bullying are related but not the same. Teasing can manifest itself in very painful ways, from verbal teasing to acts of physical aggression. A child who teases others is usually looking for attention. Some children need more attention than others, but most would rather get their attention by being listened to and understood. Teasers try to fulfill an unmet emotional need for being noticed by making others angry and upset. What better way of getting quick attention than by teasing? When teasing turns into a constant form of harassment, it becomes bullying.

> **Key Concept**
>
> *Teasing is a warning sign that should be read with caution.*

A Few Factors to Consider

There are environmental factors that can create a climate for bullying behavior. Some of these include the following:

◇ **"Proximity can deter potential problems."** When teachers are not supervising students, especially during free time and transition activities, students may see an opportunity for bullying behavior.

◇ **"The fruit doesn't fall far from the tree."** Children who come from homes where aggressive verbal and physical behavior is the norm are more likely to emulate that behavior in school.

◇ **"Peer pressure can be positive or negative."** Children can feel pressured by a peer to bully others to be part of a group or a gang. A bully's power is taken away when confronted by a united group of his or her peers who are not afraid to speak up and support the victim's right to be left alone.

◇ **"Seeing is believing."** Bullies see the world around them as being a negative environment and therefore create the world in which they "live."

◇ **"The best defense is a good offense."** It's not unusual for bullies to feel that they must hurt others before others hurt them, even though their perceived hostility usually doesn't exist.

◇ **"Out of sight, out of mind."** When teachers are asked about the problem of bullying in their schools, many say they don't see it in their classrooms so it must not be a large concern. In reality, most bullying happens on the playground or bus, and in the bathrooms, locker rooms, and hallways during transition times. It is true that bullying takes place in neighborhoods, but most bullying occurs in schools.

Who Are the Victims?

Jessica is an attractive middle school-aged girl who looks younger than many of her peers. She tries to dress fashionably and, at times, provocatively to gain the attention she feels she is lacking. She is very shy, self-conscious, and quiet in class and often goes the entire day without saying a word to her teachers. Her mother reports that she is that way at home. Jessica has a math learning disability and expresses little or no confidence in her ability to solve academic problems. She is showing interest in boys but dreads social interactions with her male classmates out of fear that she will be rejected. She socializes primarily with two other girls who sometimes complain that Jessica is "stuck up" because "she will often ignore us or walk away when we are with other students." One particular boy in her math class taunts her under his breath for the majority of the period. Sometimes other students hear his degrading comments, but most of the time Jessica is the only audience for his teasing. She says nothing when teased, trying to ignore him and hoping he will stop. But he doesn't and she continues to internalize her confusion, frustration, anger, and fear. Her parents are unaware of her distress and at school her teachers mistake her social isolation and fear of talking for her shyness and special need. Nothing will change unless a responsive adult intervenes.

Orlando is a nine-year-old boy with a quick temper and aggressive posture who has been diagnosed with Attention Deficit Hyperactivity Disorder (ADHD). He is often easily provoked by other classmates, who enjoy seeing him get upset. Most of the time, Orlando initiates his own problems with his peers by pushing, shouting, and making fun of them. Orlando has recently escalated his troublesome behavior into fighting for little or no apparent reason. He is especially adept at bothering one particularly tough kid who is also the class bully. Orlando often gets hurt in the confrontations with this bully but continues to provoke the bully in the halls and at recess.

There is a particular emotional make-up that most often defines those who are victimized by bullying behavior. Most of us have been in situations during our childhood and possibly as adults in which we felt we were being bullied. But having an occasional feeling or experience does not constitute victimization. As teachers, it is beneficial to conjure up those feelings to help us identify with those children that are dealing with bullies every day. These children are victims of bullying. An adult's empathetic feelings for a potential

> ### Key Concept
>
> *Anyone but not everyone can be a victim of bullying behavior.*

victim will serve as a catalyst for action. The following are characteristics of those who become victims of bullies:

- Passive communicators

- Physically weak

- Anxious and insecure

- Restless, hyperactive, and irritable

- Socially unskilled and isolated

- Physically or mentally disabled

- Talented and gifted

- Difficulty making friends and sustaining friendships

- Low self-esteem

- Emotionally unstable (especially males)

As you can see, there is a range of variables that may constitute a victim's personality style. Experts agree that many victims are socially unskilled and do not stand up to their bullies and that most victims fall into two categories, passive and provocative. Passive victims, such as Jessica, seem to do nothing to invite aggression and do little or nothing to defend themselves when assaulted. They never do anything to provoke their tormentor and feel unable to stop the bullying behavior, therefore rendering themselves helpless. They are non-aggressive and try to avoid confrontation at all costs. These victims often reward bullies by offering them lunch money, crying, or cowering down to bullies' demands.

The provocative group of victims are usually restless, anxious and hot-tempered. Children with Attention Deficit Hyperactivity Disorder (ADHD) can fall into this category. They tend to have poor impulse control and interpersonal skills. Because their behavior can be difficult to be around, children with ADHD can be set up to be victimized by their peers. Orlando can at times be mistaken for a bully, because he can initiate a conflict, but in reality he is no match for a bully and will ultimately lose in a confrontation.

Not all provocative victims exhibit anxious and hot-tempered behavior. Recently I mediated a bullying problem between two middle school-aged boys from different cultures. The victim (Phuong) is Vietnamese. The boy who was bullying him (Santos) took advantage of Phuong's quiet, shy demeanor, teasing and threatening him on the playground. This was brought to my attention because Phuong was seen chasing Santos and trying to trip him. But after talking with both boys and the victim's mother, it became apparent that Phuong had become a provocative victim out of frustration and insecurity.

Some children do not fall into either category. Many talented and gifted children who want to please their teachers and can be popular with others are also victimized. Some students view these children as "brown-nosers" and decide to tease them into changing their teacher-pleasing behaviors. This jealousy can be the catalyst for being bullied. The victim's academic performance will then suffer from constant bullying. They often create a fear of going to school and consequently have frequent absences.

Children who are victims in elementary school are more likely to have difficulty adjusting to middle school and high school. They avoid parts of the building where bullying may most likely occur. For example, it's not unusual to see a middle school- or high school-aged student avoiding the lunchroom and the outdoors. These are common places were bullies prey on their victims. As you can see, even at the times of day when most children look forward to relaxing and interacting with their peers, victims are fearful and avoid contact with others.

Not unlike bullies, victims have difficulties in their lives. Many child victims have academic problems in middle and high school, and studies indicate they are more likely to drop out of school. Recent studies show that 30 percent more boys than girls fall into this category. Other studies indicate that girl victims are more prone to depression. These patterns of behavior must alert us to take action by actively intervening in the lives of young people who are being victimized every day in our schools.

This book includes a variety of strategies used to intervene and change the relationship in bully-and-victim conflicts in schools. Most of the interventions for the bully, who is more proactive or deliberate in his or her aggression, aim to change the environment rather than the child. These interventions can be very effective in avoiding conflicts. Other interventions focus on changing the child, both bully and victim, by helping the bully to change the distorted thinking that makes aggression acceptable and helping the victim stick up for himself or herself.

Interventions that help provocative victims focus on decreasing and changing inappropriate behaviors for students like Orlando. Social skills awareness is an essential component of these interventions. Passive victims benefit from interventions that bring self-empowerment through awareness, modeling, rehearsing, and alternative experiences. Assertive behavior is learned, and with practice can help the victim identify his or her own special inner qualities. Chapters 3 and 4 offer a number of interventions that have proven successful for many students and teachers in today's classrooms.

Girl and Boy Bullies

When I began teaching, I quickly realized that my past perception of bullies being boys was wrong because girls are also bullies. Let's first look at the characteristics of girl bullies. In her book, *Odd Girl Out: The Hidden Culture of Aggression in Girls*, Rachel Simmons describes three types of aggressive behavior in girl bullies:

1. Uses others as pawns to indirectly hurt someone, such as spreading a false rumor

2. Tries to damage the self-esteem or status of another girl within a group

3. Uses friendship as a weapon

Girls are different than boys in that they tend to use "psychological warfare" such as ostracizing or ignoring. This can be seen as playing "mind games" with another with the intention of hurting and humiliating them into submission. In my work in an urban school district, I see the gender difference shifting as I hear and see more frequent incidents of physical confrontations between middle school- and high school-aged girls.

If no one intervenes, a girl bully will continue to dominate her classmates all through middle school and into high school. Unfortunately, it's not unusual for the adults in a girl bully's life to never seriously challenge the verbal and emotional abuse she imposes on her classmates. The quality of her relationships with others as an adult will also suffer and possibly cultivate the seeds for her children to become bullies as well.

Boy bullies tend to be much more physically aggressive than girls. They tend to exhibit these three types of aggressive behaviors:

1. Abusing others with aggressive talk or physical threats (such as "I'm going to kick your ass.")

2. Damaging others' self-esteem by using undermining comments (such as "Why don't you go to girls' gym class? You act like a pussy.")

3. Taking advantage of someone's insecurity by using them for personal gain (such as "You better bring me some money for lunch tomorrow.")

As mentioned earlier, many bullies were abused by their parents or guardians. They often have distorted thinking patterns due to poor role models and a lack of a healthy belief system. Some girls and boys try to stay friends with others who treat them cruelly. The reason, especially for girls, is that the fear of solitude can be overpowering. Many boys have been taught to be seen as "cool" and aggressive in order to succeed in school and on the streets. Being associated with "cool" and aggressive peers may be the best alternative. Having friends and getting attention from others can be an obsession for all teens. A boy seeking attention may do anything to show his power over others. A girl seeking popularity may do anything to show her loyalty to the "right" people.

Boy bullies usually grow up to become abusive husbands and fathers. Thus, it is not surprising that the children of these adults are also more likely to become bullies. Common sense tells us that both girl and boy bullying is not only a serious problem in the lives of school children, but also a major social problem in the larger culture.

Bullies in School: What Can We Do?

As we know, school can be a particularly powerful experience. A school that draws clear boundaries, guaranteeing the safety of its students, can keep bullying behavior in check. It's important that everyone who works in the school—cafeteria workers, custodial staff, paraeducators, teachers, and administrators—is made aware of the severity of the problem through workshops, memos, assemblies, school board meetings, and so on. Only then can a comprehensive intervention begin. Even though a schoolwide program is the most effective way for schools to deal with bullying, many schools have no such program. Using this book as a guide to begin effective intervention in your classroom is a positive start and can influence others to take action as well. All students must realize that bullying will not be tolerated and all victims must know how to deal with bullying behavior as well as who they can turn to for support. For crisis situations, each school community can devise a clear procedure that students and staff follow when reporting their concerns about a child who exhibits warning signs of aggressive behavior. (See Chapter 5, "Keeping Our Schools Safe," for more on this topic.)

Facilitating a Group

While the ultimate goal of any school is to protect its young people from harassment and violence, this is not always possible. However, the foundation for protecting them is laid in a schoolwide commitment to addressing bullying behavior internally and externally. A student's internal coping requires being aware of and accepting feelings and identifying a bully as well as a victim. We can help students cope with the experience externally by teaching them how and when to seek help and what methods to use for conflict resolution and problem solving. A student who feels empowered becomes less of a target of bullying behavior. If they do become a target, they can learn techniques and develop skills that will improve their situations.

Activities and strategies for helping students cope with bullying behavior can be implemented in group situations. Following is a short review of some basic principles on facilitating groups:

◇ **Access your strengths and limitations.** I have seen many teachers and other professionals become comfortable in the role of facilitator through increasing their experience and therefore comfort with this role.

◇ **Engage the entire group.** The goal is for group members to fully participate by talking more and the facilitator talking less. Young people's understanding will be deeper when they arrive at their own insights. Help them discover the points of understanding.

◇ **Provide firm guidance.** Bullying is a serious topic. Your guidance is necessary to create a classroom structure that encourages safety and maturity from all students.

Parent Partners

Parents are partners in dealing with bullying behavior at school and at home. Parents must understand the nature of the interventions being used and provide consistency at home. Always consult the parents before beginning any intervention with a child or groups of children. Chapters 3 and 4 include ways to help families of both victims and bullies. In cases in which school-based factors agitate or worsen a child's aggressive behavior, especially concerning students with special needs, the school should act to modify those factors. It appears that a disproportionate amount of children being bullied also have a learning disability, are diagnosed with ADHD, or have a mental disability. This, coupled with the trend toward full inclusion of students with special needs into our mainstream classrooms, necessitates their inclusion in strategies and programs that address bullying behavior in schools.

Most importantly, not unlike any other subject, these strategies must be taught for understanding. Putting on an anti-bullying video and answering a few questions will not have the necessary impact to alter behavior and change student attitudes.

Chapter 2

Creating a Respectful School Community

"The whole is greater than the sum of its parts."

$\mathcal{A}$ few bullies should not dictate the climate of a school's atmosphere, but bullying behavior will never change unless children, teachers, and parents become active partners in this mission against cruel behavior. This mission begins by creating a responsive school community. All educators support this premise, but not all of us understand the work and commitment necessary to achieve this goal. In these times when safety and security are our number one priority in travel and at work, it is equally important that our children feel safe and aren't fearful of being hurt in any way. An inner feeling of outer safety is a prerequisite needed before students can progress to developing a healthy sense of self. Only when our students feel physically and psychologically safe will they move beyond security to exploration, achievement, and mastery.

Creating a safe school community will make bullying behavior the exception and therefore quickly highlight its inappropriateness so school personnel can take action to stop it from reoccurring. All adults who are part of a victim's or bully's life need to have an expectation of open communication for the purpose of responding effectively to stop bullying behavior. The following scenario is an example of a school environment in which adults respond quickly:

Lee, a short, slightly built, quiet seventh-grade boy, began making up excuses about headaches and stomachaches—anything to get out of science class. Because he always liked this class and was a high-achieving student, his teacher, parents, and school nurse became concerned. After some observation and a long talk, they found the problem was not academics but physical security. Lee was being bullied.

One day a large eighth-grade boy came up to Lee, shoved him into a locker, and demanded his lunch money. He threatened to beat him up after school unless Lee gave him all his lunch money, plus a dollar every day from then to the end of the school year. The bully told Lee that he would collect the money every day outside of science class, which was before lunch. Lee complied by handing over his money the first time, but he tried to ignore the bully the next day. Again the bully slammed him around and threatened him. Lee gave him the money every day until he began making up excuses to not go to science class. The teacher, parents, and administration decided to ask Lee to go to science class so they could observe the bully harassing Lee. Lee agreed, and sure enough, as soon as the bully saw Lee, the bully approached him with a menacing look. The teacher intervened immediately and took the bully to the office.

The bully's parents were very cooperative because they understood from the beginning of the year that bullying would not be tolerated and that this school had a plan for intervening and changing the environment to a safe one. A safe school environment creates an atmosphere of trust and security where work and learning can flourish.

> **Key Concept**
>
> *Students must feel that the adult call for order and safety is more powerful than the disorder bullying can create in a school community.*

As in Lee's case, fear reduces a student's ability to concentrate on schoolwork and creates an atmosphere of mistrust. It undermines morale and conveys the impression that the school staff and parents are not in control.

How Safe Is Your School?

Adlai Stevenson once said, "My definition of a free society is a society where it is safe to be unpopular." Your students and children look to you for protection. As Abraham Maslow points out in his hierarchy of needs, people must first have their health and safety needs met before positive social interactions and achievement can occur. As a teacher, one of your responsibilities is to create environments where students can concentrate on learning, rather than on surviving real or imaginary dangers. What can you do? The following list gives an overview of steps you and your school community can take to begin creating a safer school.

1. **Be aware.** Become aware of your students' fears and concerns about their physical safety in school. Talk with them about the different areas of the school that make them feel anxious and unsafe as well as people who make them feel uneasy. The areas and people in the school that most often make students feel anxious and fearful include:

   ◇ **The empty hallways:** Students fear encountering school bullies while they are walking alone.

   ◇ **The restrooms:** This is a place where students may feel afraid of encountering other students who will "rough them up" in order to keep them from telling a teacher about drug use, smoking, harassing, and so on.

   ◇ **The school bus:** One principal of a small and relatively safe suburban elementary school told me that "on the school bus is where most of the problems occur." Students fear rowdy, aggressive, sexually inappropriate, and verbally abusive students who force them to leave a favored seat or who rough them up "just for the fun of it."

   ◇ **The unsupervised classroom:** Legally and ethically students should never be left unsupervised in a classroom, but it does occur. Teachers may need to talk briefly to someone in the hallway, take an emergency bathroom break, or be a few minutes late to class because they share classrooms. Whatever the reasons, when students are unsupervised, they fear getting into a fight with another student, being harassed, or made fun of in front of other students.

   ◇ **The principal:** Most students, even the bullies, fear going to the principal's office when discipline is the main issue.

   ◇ **Stern teachers:** Some teachers may consciously or unconsciously project a very stern persona, making them fearful just to look at. Some teachers are unpredictable in their behavior (such as a pleasant soft voice one moment and a loud screeching voice the next). This sort of behavior turns students off to relating and learning. If students get to know a teacher on a more personal level, the fear is usually dispelled.

2. **Never underestimate a student's fears.** A colleague recently reported that one of her students shared that she thought that some eighth graders were going to gang up on her after school. When asked why she thought that, she said, "because of the way they looked at me during lunch." This student's expectation of a stressful and potentially violent event can be every bit as powerful as the event itself. To reduce feelings of helplessness, students need to feel that they can turn to trusted adults, who will respond when help is needed. Students avoid asking adults for help if they feel— from their past experiences with teachers—that help is not on the way. When a student gets involved in a negative situation with another student, I ask why they didn't ask a teacher for help. Too often their response is, "I did, but they didn't do anything." We need to teach students what to do, what to say, and how to respond to other students' aggression. If necessary, we need to teach them where to turn for help should they encounter a fearful situation that is overwhelming, and when they do turn to us, we must respond accordingly.

3. **Understand.** We know that younger students who want the attention and admiration of older students may become willing victims, often giving up possessions in exchange for friendship or safety. Whatever the issue, discuss them with your students. Parents also need to become sensitive to their children's stress and struggles at school and home. I've had too many discussions with parents who feel their children (both boys and girls) should "fight it out and solve their own problems because it builds confidence and character." On the contrary, leaving a student to fight his or her own battles alone is more likely to lead to feelings of abandonment, fear, depression, low grades, and, eventually, dropping out.

Crystal, a seventh-grade student, was waiting with two other students in the hallway during class. I asked why they were in the hall, and she responded, "Because I'm waiting for Jeannie. I'm going to kick her butt." When I asked what her parents would tell her to do to resolve this problem, she responded, "My mother said not to put up with her lies and do whatever I have to do to stop her." I then asked the other two students what they thought was the best way to resolve the problem. They responded, "Mr. Khalsa, the only way Jeannie will stop spreading rumors is if she gets smacked." In this chapter you will be given ways to teach self-management skills that can prevent the cycle of students harassing other students who either cannot resolve the problem or are paralyzed with fear. Teachers sometimes need to offer their students an alternative set of values and beliefs on how to deal with problems with their peers.

Group Awareness Activities

Group Guidelines

We cannot assume that all students know how to have a discussion in a group. It is essential that you create an environment in which all students can speak without feeling threatened, insulted, or ignored. It is usually best for the students, not you, to develop shared understandings that will serve as guidelines for learning together in the classroom because when people are actively involved in making decisions, they are more apt to follow what was agreed upon.

"Group Guidelines" helps students create the necessary guidelines for group discussion and sharing. First ask students to identify one thing that someone can say or do that would be disrespectful and one thing that would be respectful. Students can either take turns sharing in a circle or write their responses on index cards. You can record the answers on a large piece of newsprint.

List the following Group Guidelines on the board. Help the group discuss each and then vote. *Thumbs-up* means it should be a class guideline and *thumbs-down* means it should not. The statements with the majority of votes become guidelines for discussion and then are posted on the wall. This list can be adapted as the year progresses.

- Talk one at a time without interrupting.

- Do not judge others.

- Stay on topic.

- Be open and honest.

- Look at the person to whom you are speaking.

- If you don't want to speak, put your head down on the desk.

- Say "I" when speaking for yourself.

- Say "you" when speaking to someone else.

- Don't make fun of what someone else says or does.

- If you want others to comment, ask "Any comments or questions?"

- Listen to what others are saying before thinking about what you want to say.

- Be supportive of others in the group.

- Everyone must share.

After deciding which statements will act as guidelines for group discussion, explain that this is the basis for a class agreement about how to work together in the classroom, sharing positive things and dealing with problems. I find it helpful to give an example for each statement. You can say: " 'Do not judge others' means not to form an opinion of someone whom you really don't know. Can someone give me an example of what not to do?" When everyone agrees with the group guidelines, have students sign or initial the agreement and post it so everyone can read it.

Who's Who

It is not unusual for some students to go through the school year in the same class and not know names or anything else about some of their classmates. One important goal of group awareness is having students get to know each other. This process often needs facilitation, especially in the middle and high school grades. It's less likely that someone will be abusive to a peer they have something in common with.

In this activity students will begin building the necessary positive relations with their peers by learning more about others in the class. Give each student a copy of page 20, "Who's Who." Ask them to circulate around the room and try to find classmates who can answer yes to the statements on the handout. When they find someone who matches one of the statements, ask them to write that person's name in the corresponding box.

The first person to fill up all the boxes calls out "Finished!" and students sit back down. Allow about 10–15 minutes for this activity. The follow-up discussion includes sharing answers and asking which statements were easiest to match and which were hardest. Bring attention to things students have in common as well.

Name _____ Date _____

Who's Who

Directions: Find someone in the group who fits each description below. Write his or her name in that appropriate square. When you have filled every box, call out "Finished!" and have a seat until everyone has completed the activity.

Plays a team sport	Doesn't like broccoli	Listens to music before going to sleep	Likes to dance
Watches cartoons	Speaks two languages	Has a younger sibling	Was born in the same month as you were
Knows a poem	Was born in another country	Has been yelled at in the past three days	Sleeps with a stuffed animal
Plays a musical instrument	Likes scary movies	Is a morning person	Is a vegetarian

What Is Bullying?

Discussing what bullying is and is not can be a touchy subject, especially when one of the students in class have been identified as having behaved in aggressive ways toward others. Regardless, it is essential that this discussion takes place and that all students feel safe to contribute. You can ask students to begin with identifying aggressive behavior that has been directed at them. This should help them to be more open to sharing the times and ways in which they have been targeted. The important thing to remember is that you may not be able to change minds immediately, but beginning the process of group understanding opens the door to progress in activities that focus on empathy.

Draw four columns on a chalkboard or large piece of newsprint. Label each column *Physical, Verbal, Emotional,* and *Sexual.* Ask students to brainstorm examples of aggressive and violent behavior. As they name examples, write them in the appropriate column. When you have at least ten responses in each column, depending on the age of your students, ask each student to come up and take turns making a "definition spiral" on another piece of newsprint. Each student chooses one word from the list and writes it as small as possible in the middle of the newsprint, adding to the list to form a spiral. Go on in this fashion until all words in the list are used. This is a visual representation of the aggressive and violent behaviors that they shared.

Questions that can be asked after this activity include:

- Are there words that can fit into more than one column?

- Where does the word *bullying* fit best?

- What kinds of behaviors in this definition spiral define *bullying*?

Give a working definition of *bullying*: Bullying is one or more individuals using threats of bodily harm, assault, or battery to cause physical, verbal, or emotional harm on another individual. Simply stated, bullying is any behavior that is hurtful to someone else's physical, emotional, or mental self, regardless if the person intended it to be hurtful or not.

Now that your students have a working definition of bullying, this activity can help them understand more about bullying behavior. Introduce the following concepts and write them on the board to keep students focused:

- A bully needs a victim.

- A bully likes to feel stronger and better than others.

- A bully uses his or her power to hurt others.

Next, ask students to answer the six true or false questions on the "What Is Bullying?" handout (p. 23). Follow up the activity by checking their answers and holding a group discussion:

1. **FALSE.** Bullying is not just teasing. Both teasers and bullies want attention, but bullies take it to another level. Teasing can be fun at times. Bullying can begin with name-calling but will turn from verbal teasing to possible acts of physical violence. Remember, teasers want attention and like to "fool around," but bullies try to exercise control over other students by verbally or physically assaulting them.

2. **TRUE.** Anyone can become a victim of bullying and many of us have been in a situation in which we felt we were bullied, but certain types of behavior and personalities will increase the chances of someone becoming a victim of bullying. Victims can learn how to deal with bullies, but first they must learn that they can depend on adults for help.

3. **FALSE.** Boys use different bullying tactics than girls. Boys are more physical and observable. However, girls also bully, using tactics such as intimidation, spreading rumors, and verbal abuse.

4. **TRUE.** The single most effective deterrent to bullying is adult authority. Students need to know that they alone do not have to solve the problem of being bullied. Once they know that, they can learn techniques to deal with bullies.

5. **FALSE.** Ignoring bullying behavior is usually ineffective. Bullies are often determined to control their victims. One of the most effective ways of stopping bullies is to avoid confrontation, which might mean walking the other way. This form of "ignoring" is effective.

6. **FALSE.** Most adults walking down a street who notice some tough-looking guys at the end of the block wouldn't think, "I'll just walk right by them to show I'm not afraid." The wise thing to do would be to think of options and avoid the potential danger. Avoiding a bully because you don't want to get hurt or be put in an uncomfortable situation is not a sign of weakness. It's good common sense.

Name _____   Date _____

What Is Bullying?

Directions: Read each statement below. Decide if each is true or false. Circle your answer.

1. Bullying is teasing.   True   False

2. Anyone can become a victim.   True   False

3. Bullies are usually boys.   True   False

4. It's best to tell an adult if you're being bullied.   True   False

5. Bullies will stop if you ignore them.   True   False

6. Showing a bully you're afraid by avoiding them
   is a sign of weakness.   True   False

How Do Bullies Behave?

The purpose of this activity is to help your students identify the behaviors associated with bullying. We understand that bullies try to exercise control over their peers but it's equally important to help students understand that bullying includes a wide range of inappropriate and abnormal behaviors. This activity requires students to generate a "Bullying Behaviors List." As they brainstorm behaviors, write them on a large piece of newsprint and post it on the classroom wall. These behaviors can include the following:

- Make verbal threats

- Boss people around

- Harass people

- Take people's money

- Put people down

- Make obscene gestures

- Pick or hurt people because of their sexual preference, race, religion, culture, etc.

- Attack people physically

- Intimidate people

- Act like they are more important than everyone

- Gossip

- Leave people out

- Spread rumors

- Tease

- Curse

- Hit

- Hurt

- Refuse to work things out in a respectful way

After generating a list of behaviors, ask students to give an example next to each behavior. For example: "Gossip"—"Did you hear, Joe likes Cindy."

Talking about Bullying

Ask your students to think about a time when they were either bullied, witnessed someone getting bullied, heard about someone who was bullied, or bullied someone else. Then hand out pages 26 and 27 and ask students to answer the questions by writing a paragraph describing their experiences. It's important that every student understands that he or she *should not use anyone's name when telling the story.*

Working with a classmate, students can now share their bullying experiences. One partner will first be the listener while the other is the speaker, and then they will change roles. Be aware of which students are working together, avoiding partners that are already having interpersonal problems.

After the pairs of students share their stories (5–10 minutes), allow time for a few volunteers to share one experience with the class. Facilitate a group discussion by asking questions such as the following:

- Why do some people avoid helping others who are being bullied?

- Why do some people do something about being bullied?

- How does it feel to hear other classmates' stories?

- What may you do in the future that you didn't do in the past?

- What advice would anyone like to give someone in the group?

Name _____ Date _____

Talking about Bullying

Directions: Answer the questions below.

1. Write about a time when you were bullied by another student.

_____

_____

_____

_____

2. Write about a time when you saw someone else being bullied. What did you do?

_____

_____

_____

_____

3. Write about a time when you heard about someone in your school being bullied. What did you do?

_____

_____

_____

_____

Name _____   Date _____

Talking About Bullying (continued)

4. Write about a time when you said or did something that was hurtful to someone else.

_____

_____

_____

_____

Draw what you think a bully looks like:

Weekly Check-in

First and foremost, young people need to know that school staff are available to help them understand any insecurity or fear that they may be experiencing in school. This activity gives students the opportunity to review the events of a given week at school and gain an awareness of the significance of those events.

Some students may resist filling out this weekly report (see page 30). Their mistrust to divulge weekly experiences usually arises out of the way they have been treated in the past. It has been my experience that both well-adjusted students and students with problematic behaviors can benefit from this activity. I encourage you to not let difficult or problematic behaviors disqualify a student from participating. After all, consider the purpose of this activity. Here is an opportunity for you to reach and help those students who are hesitant for one reason or another to open up and share their thoughts and experiences of school.

Before asking students to fill out this weekly check-in:

◇ Read the directions out loud and ask if anyone has any questions before starting.

◇ Encourage students to fill out as much of the report as they feel comfortable doing.

◇ Make positive comments about students who are motivated to participate. Use them as exemplars, but do so in a subtle way so that you do not separate them from the "unmotivated students," therefore creating a destructive competition between students.

◇ Use past success to illustrate the possible benefits of filling out the weekly check-in ("After a few students in another class filled this out, they realized that they were avoiding a big problem that affected their whole day. Things improved after dealing directly with the issues they were not aware of. I'm sure some of you may get this same benefit.")

◇ Before all the students have completed filling out their reports, briefly interrupt the activity and review your expectations. Praise those who are staying focused on the activity.

After collecting their reports, you can get a clearer understanding of how many students in your classroom are being bullied or are at risk of being harassed by a peer. Initiate personal contact with each student and find out how each felt about filling out the report. Begin a discussion with those who said they were having problems with another student or were bothering other students. Some of this conversation can take place in a group. You may wish to have at least one individual session with students who are difficult to reach.

You can also use the weekly check-in to gather information that you may need to share with school administrators and parents. It's not unusual for a student to change his or her mind or deny reporting events that he or she said happened in the past. These reports will establish a history of experiences that may be important to review in the future.

Choose a Feeling

Feelings are often misinterpreted or misunderstood. Part of understanding one's feelings is being able to identify, label correctly, and accept one's own feelings during both positive and negative experiences.

Hand out page 31. Instruct students to read aloud the words in the box at the top of the page, discussing the meaning of each feeling word. Then ask them to write the word in each blank that they think best fits the situation described.

Afterward, hold a class discussion, asking students to compare their choices and the reasons behind those choices.

Weekly Check-in

Directions: This Weekly Check-in helps us understand how your week was in school. Read each statement and check the box that best indicates what happened. When finished, give this to your teacher.

✓ This week someone:	Never	One time	More Than Once
1. Gave me a compliment			
2. Was helpful			
3. Said mean things to me			
4. Tried to physically hurt me			
5. Stood up for me			
6. Threatened me			
7. Made fun of me			
8. Tried to take my money			
9. Shared something with me			
10. Refused to talk to me			
11. Tried to make me hurt someone			
12. Tried to get me in trouble			
13. Spread rumors about me			
14. Hit me			
15. Got others to hurt me			
16. Had fun with me			

Name _____   Date _____

Choose a Feeling

Directions: First read all the feeling words and discuss their meaning with a partner or the class. Next write the feeling word that best matches the situation in each situation described below.

WORD BANK

sad	fear	happy	peaceful	angry	loving
apprehensive		excited	frustrated	anxious	nervous

---

1. You were just told that the family will be going to Hawaii for winter vacation.

   _____

2. You found out that your best friend might have told a lie about you.

   _____

3. The party you've been waiting to go to has been canceled.

   _____

4. Someone said they saw you steal money that you did not steal.

   _____

5. You're sitting next to a lake, reading a favorite book on a sunny day.

   _____

6. You've been told that you passed a very important exam.

   _____

7. You've been told that the class bully is mad at you.

   _____

Dealing with Feelings

Understanding how events affect feelings is only the first step. Your students need to respond by acting in a manner that solves problems. I tell my students that "life's situations either control you or you control life's situations." This activity helps students explore emotionally mature decisions during challenging times.

You cannot keep students from having feelings, but you can choose what types of interactions you will support in the classroom. If you tend to be "teacher-centered," then your concentration will be on subject matter and not on open expressions of feelings in the classroom. The fear of control loss is one of the roots of establishing a more student- or group-centered approach toward teaching. A teacher-centered approach has its consequences. Students will feel a lack of control and ability to say what is on their minds.

I suggest working toward a student-centered approach in the classroom. We want our students to generate interpersonal feelings as well as intellectual responses to facts and concepts. Denying appropriate open expression of feelings is as harmful to learning as it would be to prohibit any discussion about writing during language arts class. Improving communication is a foundational skill for creating a school that responds quickly. Dealing effectively with bullying behavior requires students to express and deal with their feelings in an open and productive manner. Unexpressed feelings can lead to a stressful climate that denies self-direction and consequently inhibits learning. Understanding and expressing feelings is a skill that can be taught. Here are some suggestions for modeling the expression of feelings:

◇ Greet your students every day with a smile, a hello, and a comment such as, "Max, good to see you. How are you feeling this morning?"

◇ Place a large piece of newsprint on an easel in the front of the class. Upon entering the classroom, each student is asked to answer the questions on the newsprint:

1. "Today I'm feeling _____ because _____."

2. "Today I'm feeling _____ because _____."

◇ Post "feeling words" next to the easel or on a wall where all students can refer to it.

◇ Do not hesitate to clearly state how you're feeling during the day's interactions.

Name _____ Date _____

Dealing with Feelings

Directions: Fill out this worksheet and then discuss your answers with a partner or the class.

Situation: What happened?	How did it make you feel?	What could you do?
Someone demanded that you give him your lunch money.		
You lost a ring your mother let you borrow.		
Your pet died and your brother or sister doesn't seem to care.		
A friend spread a bad rumor about you.		
You just found out that your parents are separating.		
Someone is threatening to fight you after school.		
You've been told that you'll probably fail a class.		

Changing Thoughts

Once you have introduced your students to activities that ask them to use feeling words, it's very important that they understand the source of their feelings. The key to understanding feelings is understanding how one's mind works. Ask your students to sit and think about the last time they were having a lot of fun. Ask them to think about what they were doing and how it felt. Then ask them how they are feeling in the present moment. Many students will most likely say they are feeling very good. Then point out that they are still in the classroom, so what has changed? What created the new improved feelings? The answer is their thoughts.

I was talking to a student after school and our discussion went like this:

Student: "I was really depressed today."

Mr. Khalsa: "Why were you having so many depressing thoughts?"

Student: "I wasn't having depressing thoughts; I was just *feeling* depressed all day."

This student did not understand the fundamental principle of how feelings and thoughts work together. Feelings follow and respond to every thought we have, regardless of how short or long a period of time we think those thoughts. For example, say this student had the following thought at the start of the day: "My teachers really don't care if I pass or not." That student became depressed about school as soon as that thought came to mind. The student did not realize or understand that he created the depressed feeling with a "depressed thought." I helped him understand the effects of negative thinking by using food as an analogy: If he ate something that tasted spoiled and he had a bad taste in his mouth, he wouldn't wonder why he had the bad taste in his mouth because he was aware of who put the food in his mouth. I explained that thinking is no different. He began his day with depressed thoughts and that caused the depressed feelings throughout the day.

Students who are being harassed have constant fearful and anxious thoughts and live in fear. To help your students get control of their feelings, help them understand that they are the thinkers of their thoughts and *to change a feeling, they need to change their thinking.*

To begin, hand out page 35. Instruct students to read each statement and, in the center column, write the word that best expresses what they felt while reading the statement. Have them underline the words in the statement that brought up that feeling. In the last column, have them write any new thoughts or feelings they have about the statement.

Name _____   Date _____

Changing Thoughts

Directions: Read each sentence and write the feeling it creates. Then underline the words that created the feeling. Next, write a new thought and possible new feelings that the new thought created.

	Feeling(s)	**New Thought and Feeling(s)**
1. You have to <u>move</u> and transfer <u>to a different school.</u>		
2. You drop your books, look up, and see a student smiling at you.		
3. Your friend tells you he or she can't meet you after school because something "came up."		
4. A movie you've been waiting to see is no longer playing in theaters.		
5. Your father tells you he can't come to your basketball game.		

A True Friend?

When a student feels lonely and is unable to make real friends, he or she may decide to become a bully. A victim usually feels isolated from others and may lack the skills to make friends as well. All students can benefit from learning what it takes to make friends. Making friends comes easy for some students and is a mystery for others. Start by sharing what it was like for you when you were their age and wanted to make friends with others. Discuss the following list of skills and basic awarenesses that you needed to learn to make and keep friends:

◇ **Newton's Law:** Every action has an equal and opposite reaction. Most of the time when you are kind to someone, he or she will be kind back. The opposite is also true, so think before you say or do something.

◇ **Two Ears for Listening:** Our bodies were made with one mouth and two ears. Maybe that's because listening is more important than talking all the time. Pay attention to what others say to you by looking in their eyes and not thinking about what you want to say.

◇ **Loose Lips Sink Ships:** Most problems occur when "he said, she said" occurs between students in school. Once you say something negative about someone, it is impossible to take back and will sink any possibility of making friends with that person.

◇ **It's Better to Hold Hands Than to Point Fingers:** Holding hands can be a metaphor for thinking of someone before yourself. Instead of trying to blame someone for a problem that may need cooperation to solve, try to find common ground with the other person.

◇ **Share Your Strengths:** Friendship is built on mutual likeness and attraction. Often we are attracted to basic likes and dislikes. For example: sports, music, culture, clothes, subjects, religion, goals, food, and so on. In order to find out who may have something in common with you, share what you like and what you do well (without being a show-off).

◇ **Protect Yourself:** Sometimes in our desire to have friends we take to much verbal, emotional and sometimes physical abuse from others to be liked. Protect yourself. Some people aren't really good friends at all.

To begin the activity, hand out page 37. Instruct students to read each statement and decide if it is true or false. They then write **T** or **F** in the corresponding blank. When they are finished, they can discuss their answers with a partner or the class.

Name _____   Date _____

A True Friend?

Directions: Read each statement and decide if it is true or false. Then write **T** or **F** in the corresponding blank. Discuss your answers with a partner or the class.

1. A true friend always agrees with you. _____

2. A true friend has a lot in common with you. _____

3. A true friend stands up for you. _____

4. A true friend listens to you. _____

5. A true friend will tell you what he or she thinks. _____

6. A true friend always keeps secrets. _____

7. A true friend shares what he or she has. _____

8. A true friend can be bossy. _____

9. A true friend teases a lot. _____

10. A true friend admits being wrong. _____

11. A true friend likes everything you like. _____

12. A true friend knows what bothers you. _____

Building Appreciation for Differences

Today's teachers are required to have an understanding, awareness, and sensitivity to the diverse needs in their classes. Studies show that teachers who spend some time, helping students to get to know each other see a decrease in acting-out behavior and bullying. Empathy builds important human bridges between student and student, student and teacher, student and class. Plan some activities that support positive group interaction and cooperation. Let your students know that these activities can be fun, but more important, they can change the climate in the classroom to one of cooperation and support.

Examples:

⬥ **Student of the Week:** This activity has been available to all teachers for years but unfortunately I rarely see it being used. Post a large piece of newsprint in front of the class. Ask students to sit in a circle. Choose one student every week to be The Student of the Week. Take the student's photo and put it on the top section of the newsprint with a list of attributes underneath it. Give every other student an opportunity to say something they like or admire about the Student of the Week. Remind students that when it is their turn, they are going to want others to say something positive about them, so they should do the same. They can list their comments under the photo and then take turns looking at The Student of the Week and telling him or her what they wrote. The Student of the Week should then say, "thank you." This part of the activity can be uncomfortable for some students, but the skill it teaches is very important. Teach your students how to give descriptive compliments. For example: "Sara has a great smile," versus "She's a nice person."

⬥ **Group Projects:** Any group project is productive that encourages cooperation as students work toward a common goal. For example, divide the class into groups of three or four. You can let students form their own groups or manipulated groups by putting students who may have little in common in the same group. Give each group a box of plastic straws and masking tape. The goal is to see which group can design and construct the highest straw tower. This activity can take twenty to thirty minutes. Your role is to monitor the groups, making sure everyone has a responsibility and is given a chance to construct part of the straw tower.

◇ **Rewarding Cooperation:** Do not miss an opportunity to point out when your students are cooperating. Giving certificates, privileges, and bonuses can all act as incentives to keep the cooperative momentum going. Point out the intrinsic values contained in the cooperative activity. Point to "Thinking Signs" around the room that support your message. For example, "There is no I in Team" or "When we cooperate, everyone wins."

◇ **Anti-bullying Posters:** I've worked with classes that designed anti-bullying posters for the school and wrote a skit to perform in other classes as well. This show of unity can be a very powerful change agent. It invites other students to think about bullying in their school community. You can use this poster campaign as an introduction to helping students discuss their issues with bullying and what can be done to stop it.

◇ **What's Different?:** This activity is a favorite among students of all ages. Begin with a discussion about what makes people similar and what makes them different. Helping students focus on internal similarities will support the cooperative climate that is essential for security and safety. For example, they all want to make friends, gain the skills being taught, be respected and feel part of the school community. Acknowledge external differences as well but only to point out personal tastes, trends, and so on. To start the activity, ask students to sit in a large circle. Have a volunteer walk around the classroom as all the students observe what he or she is wearing, from head to feet. Ask the volunteer to step outside the classroom for a few minutes and change one small thing about his or her dress—for example, an earring, a rolled-up sleeve, a tucked-in shoelace, and so on. This student should then come back in and walk around the classroom while other students take turns guessing what changed. Whoever guesses correctly is the next volunteer.

◇ **Avoid Grade Competition:** I have found that many students are anxious about their grades and would rather not have papers posted around the room. In saying that, I think showing exemplars of what is expected can help all students reach that standard. Some teachers make a point of finding work that the anxious student will give permission to display, thereby gradually desensitizing the student to others' feedback.

Teaching Conflict Resolution

With differences come conflict. All people at some time will need help resolving minor or major conflicts. Yet we usually perceive conflict as a negative occurrence rather than as an opportunity for change and personal growth. Your students will need skills and guidance to achieve successful conflict resolution. There are a wide variety of conflict resolution curricula and programs that are very effective and can be implemented at all school levels. The following simple guide stems from my practical experience working with two or more students who are having a conflict.

There are two prerequisites that must occur for successful conflict resolution. First, both students need to want to try and solve the problem together. If they are not ready to do this, wait until they are. Second, you must feel comfortable handling the conflict. Being an effective mediator requires the teacher or student to understand the process and maintain a neutrality, regardless of who is "right or wrong."

Setting the Stage

Successful conflict resolution starts with the following steps. Setting the stage in this manner will help build trust between all participants and give each of the disputants a clear understanding of what to expect and how to act during the mediation process.

1. Get an agreement from those involved on whether they would like your help solving the problem.

2. Find a private place to do the mediation.

3. Explain that this process is an alternative to the punitive option. If they cannot work out a solution to their problem, then you may not have a choice but to refer it to the vice principal.

4. Explain that you won't take sides or tell them how to solve the problem but may suggest ways to proceed.

5. Ask students to agree that they will:
   - try their best to solve the problem without any personal attacks
   - listen to each other by not interrupting when the other person is speaking
   - be as honest as they can

Six-step Mediation Process

1. **What Happened?** Ask each student to take turns describing what specific events occurred that led up to the conflict. After each student is finished, restate what they said to make certain everyone understands what was said. You may want to ask "How did you feel?" This helps each student gain a deeper understanding of what happened and how it affected each. Praise each student for being honest.

2. **How Does the Other Feel and Why?** In order for a resolution to occur, both students must express a degree of empathy for the other person. Ask each student to restate how the other person feels and why.

3. **Summarize the Whole Problem.** Often we do not spend enough time on this step but instead jump to brainstorming solutions to the conflict. You may want to ask, "Is there anything else?" Then summarize the problem, including key facts and feelings both students shared. You can identify any common concerns both students expressed as well.

4. **Brainstorm Solutions.** It's important that the students help generate possible solutions. If they are stuck, ask, "What advice would you give someone who was feeling like the other student? Can you think of something else you could do? Why is this a good solution?"

5. **Decide on a Solution.** Make certain that the agreed-upon solution works for both of them. Ask, "What can you do differently if this happens again?" Praise mature responses.

6. **Evaluate Progress.** I always ask both students to agree on returning in a few days at a designated place and time to evaluate how the conflict resolution is working. Most students look forward to returning and reporting on their progress. Congratulate them on a successful mediation experience. If after a few days the solution is not getting the desired results, return to the mediation process and discuss what needs to change and why.

Class Meetings and Problem Solving

This is an alternative approach to addressing issues happening in and out of the classroom. This system has been used primarily at the elementary and middle school levels. At the end of each day, ask any student who participated in mediation that day, "Has your problem been resolved during the day?" Provide a clipboard with a copy of the Problem Board Form on page 43, which asks the student to write his or her name, the person with whom he or she is in conflict, and a brief explanation of what happened. If the problem has not been resolved by the end of the day, he or she can share the situation in a formal meeting with the class, and the class can decide on the consequence upon consensus.

You can also have regularly scheduled classroom meetings for a designated amount of time. For example, every Monday and Friday for 15 minutes each. Before having a problem solved by the class, you may want to ask that the students need to try at least one strategy for solving the problem before they are allowed to enter it on the board. During the class meetings, the person being accused of being involved has an opportunity to respond. Screen the problems recorded and handle those situations that are inappropriate for this format in alternative ways.

Problem Board Form

Name:	Conflict with:	What happened?
_____	_____	_____
_____	_____	_____
_____	_____	_____
_____	_____	_____
_____	_____	_____
_____	_____	_____
_____	_____	_____
_____	_____	_____
_____	_____	_____
_____	_____	_____
_____	_____	_____

Teacher–Student Communication

In the real estate business the three most important things to consider are location, location, and location. When creating a school community that responds quickly to student issues, the three most important factors are relationship, relationship, and relationship. Knowing your students can help you understand the problems they are having in their daily lives. The average student who is bullied will keep it to himself or herself. The student may fear that an adult won't understand or believe him or her. Relationship building starts with the basics, which you're probably doing: greeting them as they enter the classroom, letting them know you're happy to see them after a weekend or vacation, complimenting them on their clothing or accomplishment other areas, and so on. All too often, many teachers incorrectly assume that by doing these "essentials," they don't need to do much else to get to know their students. For example, a teacher might greet all of her students as they enter the classroom, but if one student doesn't raise his head and respond, does that warrant more time with the student? We know that some students may need to be left alone and approached at another time, while others need the issue addressed as soon as it occurs. Here are more ideas that are among my favorites.

Conferences

I believe that all students should have the opportunity to meet with one of their teachers on a one-on-one basis. This meeting can be a personalized period of time when you and your student sit face-to-face and discuss school life.

> **Key Concept**
>
> *Academics can become a major component of a conference, but so can the student's social life, which, if you ask, is the most meaningful part of their day.*

One of the major challenges in all classrooms can be finding time to schedule a conference. Recently, one teacher shared that by meeting with her students one-to-one once every few months, she actually saved time that probably would have been used dealing with the "mountains" that were once only "molehills." You can find out so much about your students with just a five-minute conference. When discussing an academic subject, interviewing the student about schoolwork can have a positive impact. For example, in reading, ask the student some basic questions about his or her book. In writing, have the student read a composition to you and get feedback on what they liked, are not sure of, and so on. For social issues, some students may need some prompting to talk about problems that they're dealing with. You can ask the student to first ask you a question and then you'll ask them a question.

Some students do not need prompting to start a conversation but instead need direction and focus. A mini-agenda would be useful for these students. (See Chapter 4, "Helping the Bullies," for steps for conducting a one-on-one problem-solving meeting.) Whatever form the conference takes, you'll find that the rewards of this sharing time far outweigh the challenges of scheduling.

Checking-in Box

The Checking-in Box is another writing activity that can give you some insight into your students' weekly experiences at school. Your students can never write too much. Journaling can be a method of helping your students keep their thoughts and problems in a book. Put a box with a lid and a slit on top in a distinctive place in the classroom. You or your students can decorate it and label it the "Checking-in Box."

Explain this activity by saying to students: "Writing about your daily experiences can be the most enjoyable and motivating form of writing. I will have Checking-in Box forms for you to use. Once a week I'll ask you to spend some time answering the questions on the form and then putting them in the box before you leave. You can write as much or as little as you want and will not be graded for your work. This activity is another way we can talk with each other and therefore help each other have a successful year."

Page 46 shows a blank form. You can fill in your own questions. Some possible questions are the following:

- What are three successes you had this week?

- Talk about a problem you solved this week.

- What is a challenge you're dealing with?

- What do you wish had never happened this week?

- How could you have improved your week and why?

- What was something that made you laugh this week?

- Talk about something that is worrying you.

- What are your plans for the weekend?

After reading the forms, you may want to write comments that can help each student understand that you understand. Comments can also include scheduling appointments for students that may need to meet and discuss a problem further with you.

Checking-in Box

Directions: After reading the question below, write down your thoughts. Remember this form is not going to be graded or criticized in any way, but I will use it to help us communicate.

Question: _____

_____

Your Thoughts: _____

_____

_____

_____

_____

_____

_____

_____

_____

"I" and "You" Messages

Students must learn what to say and how to say it if they are to establish positive social relationships with their peers. Students with ineffective communication skills often experience difficulty asserting themselves and developing meaningful friendships. The following activities are designed to help students develop effective strategies for communicating with others so they can use language to establish relationships, to communicate their thoughts and feelings effectively in social situations, and to solve problems that they encounter in their daily school life experiences.

Knowing Yourself —Warm-up Quotes: Use the following quotes to "set the stage" in helping students explore the importance of knowing themselves. State each quote and then follow up with the questions below.

"Friendship with oneself is all important, because without it one cannot be friends with anyone else."—*Eleanor Roosevelt*

- Why did Eleanor Roosevelt believe that if you can't be friends with yourself you'll have a difficult time being friends with others?

- How does someone become friends with themselves?

- Why can it be difficult?

- What can you do to help someone else become friends with themselves?

"Things aren't the way they are, but the way you are."—*Anonymous*

- Does this quote make sense? Why? Why not?

- What does this quote say about the importance of how you think?

- Give me an example of when you saw something one way and someone else interpreted it a totally different way.

- How important is your attitude? Why?

Using "I" Messages: Explain to your students that it is important to know how to assert yourself, especially when someone is bothering you. One way of asserting yourself is to use an "I" message when you want to tell someone what is bothering you about their behavior.

An "I" message expresses what I feel, what's happened to make me feel that way, and what I need. Explain that we use "I" messages to speak only for ourselves and not for or about others. "I" messages reduce tension and can stop the escalation of conflict because they allow the other student to save face and to understand what you are really feeling. It takes courage to speak in this way when you are upset or angry, but if done correctly "I" messages will often get the results you want.

Post these examples of true and false "I" messages on the board or hand them out for all students to read:

True "I" Messages:

- I feel mad when you tell everyone things that I told you privately. I want to be able to share things with you and know you will not share them with anyone else.

- I feel scared when you pretend to throw things at me when we are alone or outside. I want to be able to see you without being concerned that you might hurt me.

- When you ask me for lunch money, I feel uneasy because I only have enough money for myself. I need you to stop asking me for money.

- I feel angry and embarrassed when you make fun of my weight. I'd like you to keep your negative comments to yourself.

False "I" Messages:

- I think you are doing this to annoy me, and that's obnoxious.

- I think she better give me my CD back.

- I think he is wrong and is a real jerk for doing that.

- When you took my book, I wanted to smack you. If you do it again, I just might.

- I think you're asking for big trouble and I know who can give it to you.

- I'm afraid to go there with you because you're mean.

Helping your students understand how communication can create or destroy safe classrooms will be beneficial to bullies, their victims, and others who want to stand up for their rights. Communication has two parts; what is said and what is heard. Learning assertiveness skills by using effective "I" messages can give every student the right to stand up to people who tease, criticize, put us down, or are just inconsiderate of the feelings of others.

We know that it is not sufficient to just tell your students how to look and act assertive but, as in academics, these skills need to be practiced. One elementary school teacher makes it a point in her daily routine to include having all her students practice looking at each other while giving a respectful greeting. She shared, "If I don't expect them to practice these basic social skills, they will fall back into their old habits, which are usually unproductive. If I expect them to act a certain way, I must also inspect their progress daily." If this sounds familiar, take a few minutes every morning with your elementary or middle school students to practice, role-play, and evaluate basic assertiveness skills that are required for effective communication with peers and teachers.

Name _____ Date _____

"I" and "You" Messages

Directions: Read the statements below. Put an "I" next to all "I" messages and a "You" next to all "You" messages. Then change all "You" messages to "I" messages.

_____ **1.** I need you to just get out of my way and leave me alone!

_____ **2.** Why don't you start changing the way you act?

_____ **3.** You are so annoying when you tease me!

_____ **4.** I think school should be a safe place to learn and make friends.

_____ **5.** Be quiet. You talk too much.

_____ **6.** Don't tell me it's no problem. You don't know how I feel.

_____ **7.** I felt bad about not asking you to join us yesterday.

_____ **8.** I don't like it when you stare at me. It makes me feel weird and I'd like you to stop.

_____ **9.** Why don't you pick on someone else for a change?

_____ **10.** I'm not interested in your problems so go bug someone else.

_____ **11.** You'd better get out of my chair before I get angry.

_____ **12.** You never listen when I talk to you!

_____ **13.** Sometimes I feel scared going into the bathroom without a friend with me.

_____ **14.** You should just leave me alone.

_____ **15.** Why are you treating me different than you treat the others?

Assertive Body Language

Body language is a large part of our words. It often speaks louder than the words we say or hear. I've included activities that will help your students become aware of and then understand how to avoid the "passive/victim trap" by rehearsing to look assertive. Hand out page 52.

Body Language Match Game

To start this activity, divide the class into groups of three or four and give each group a set of Match Cards (pp. 53 and 54). Have students cut out cards and place them facedown on the table. One at a time, players turn over cards to try and match drawings and words. Play continues until all cards have been matched and the player with the most cards is the winner.

How Did They Do?

This activity helps students use the skills they have learned in the previous activities. Effective communication, unlike academics, needs practice, understanding, and the ability to use it in real-life situations.

To begin, have students pair up. Then give each pair a copy of pp. 55 and 56. Instruct students to look at each of the pictured scenarios on the handouts and discuss how the student handled each situation. Afterward, hold a class discussion about students' thoughts.

Assertive Body Language

Saying what you mean without trying to hurt another person's feelings is called being *assertive*. When you keep things inside and don't say what is on your mind, you are being *passive*. If someone tells another person what they think but is hurtful and blaming, they are using aggressive talk. Bullies often are *aggressive* and don't think about others' feelings.

What does an assertive person look like?

- Stands straight when talking

- Looks into the other person's eyes

- Keeps his or her hands at the sides or in pockets

- Keeps a comfortable distance, usually two feet, from the other person

Directions: Using the guidelines above, in the space below or on another piece of paper, draw what you think an assertive person looks like. You can also label the different parts of the "assertive body language."

Body Language Match Game

Body Language Match Cards

SAD	PASSIVE	CONFUSED
AFRAID	ASSERTIVE	ANGRY
HAPPY	NERVOUS	DISGUSTED
LONELY	HOPEFUL	AGGRESSIVE

Body Language Match Game (continued)

Body Language Match Cards

How Did They Do?

Directions: How did the student handle these situations in which another student tried to tease or intimidate him or her? Work with a partner to decide if he or she handled the situation well, and, if so, what skills did he or she use?

The Buddy System

Some students will need a partner or buddy to support their ability and desire to feel part of the classroom and school community. The buddy system can be used to help a potential victim of being bullied gain the understanding and security to deal with an uncomfortable or dangerous situation.

Creating a Buddy System

◇ **The Witness:** Many of us experienced the witness buddy system when we were young and at the local pool. You didn't get into the pool without your buddy, and when the whistle blew, you and your buddy found each other. You and your swim buddy were there to watch over each other, to make sure you both knew where the other one was. This system helped you feel safe and your parents feel more confident in letting you swim without their needing to watch over you.

Having bullies around can take the fun out of school. Some students feel afraid to go to the lunchroom, the bathroom, or the playground because they fear being harassed by bullies. The witness buddy system can be used in school as well. Often a new student is assigned a "volunteer buddy" to show him or her around, make introductions, sitting together at lunch, and so on. If you know of a student who is being harassed or picked on and needs additional help in feeling safe in school, assign or ask for a "volunteer buddy" to be with this student when walking to school, to class, sitting together at lunch, being aware of each other at recess and walking to the bus together. It is often best to change buddies every other day and to set up time at the end of each day to discuss how it is working.

◇ **The Informal Mentor:** This buddy system addresses the need to help a student who needs support in applying the "What to Do About Bullying" skills. The mentor buddy is another student(s) who has gained the skills necessary for effectively dealing with a bully. (These skills are covered in Chapter 3.) This type of buddy system requires that students are willing and able to mentor others. You'll need to also document progress as well as setbacks that occur along the way. The documentation doesn't need to be kept in a huge binder. Simply keeping an ongoing journal will suffice.

When you first assign a buddy, he or she will act as a guide. The mentor buddy should explain that one doesn't have to let bullying get the best of you and there are things to try if you are bothered by a bully. The buddy is available to answer questions about anything that may be difficult or confusing to the student being helped. You may choose to end the buddy relationship after everyone thinks the student in need of support is ready to deal with the issues in school more independently.

Potential Problems

Even if you put in a lot of planning in a mentoring buddy system, things may not work out so well. Here are some common problems that may come up:

⬦ **The buddy assigned ends up not wanting to be a buddy.** Some students don't feel comfortable taking on the responsibility for helping another student. There should be no pressure put on them to be a buddy even if you feel they would be helpful and are ready. Maybe you can find other ways for that student to be helpful to others.

⬦ **The buddy is overprotective of the victim.** Try not to allow a buddy to short-circuit the victim's learning experience. The buddy probably has good intentions, but the victim doesn't get the opportunity to handle situations that may be growth-producing.

⬦ **The buddy stops being a buddy before the victim is ready.** It's important to make a list of milestones to be reached before the buddy system ends. That way everyone will have clear feedback about how well things are progressing.

In summary, creating a buddy system needs to be handled with care. Make certain with feedback from other colleagues that you have chosen a buddy who is willing. Create a simple method of documentation that can help you and others determine the success of this support system and watch for potential problems so you can guide both students in their work together.

Creating Respectful Schools

A respectful school begins with creating respectful classrooms. A respectful classroom may mean different things to different people. One teacher may think it is disrespectful if a student she's reprimanding doesn't look her in the eye. Another teacher may think a student should look at the ground and just listen during a reprimand. We can all agree, however, that students in a respectful classroom all feel physically and emotionally safe and valued for who they are. Students who do not feel safe will find it difficult to learn and establish meaningful relationships in school.

It's imperative that you notice interactions between students, follow up to learn why something unusual has occurred, and do not tolerate harassment of any kind. But creating respectful classrooms also depends on the degree of respect that has been established in the hallways, bathrooms, cafeteria, and playground and on the buses. Even in the safest classroom, students will not feel safe if they have to deal with abuse and harassment to get from class to class. Bullies are aware of the times they can and cannot use their power of intimidation. After discussing this problem with high school students, I was surprised to find out how some of them found ways to "survive" in their unsafe schools. Some students where driven to drawing up a floor plan of the school to identify the safest and fastest way to get out of the building and then reenter at the closest point to their next class, therefore avoiding walking through the hallways. When I asked a high school class of students with special learning needs about the major cause of stress in their school day, most of them responded, "Walking in the hallways."

> **Key Concept**
>
> *The teacher is the key. A respectful classroom requires a teacher who does not tolerate harassment or social exclusion.*

A respectful and safe classroom that enables every student to focus on academics and positive social interactions can exist in a school that has safe and respectful hallways, cafeterias, buses, and so on. You cannot single-handedly ensure all students' safety throughout the whole school, but you can bring your classroom close to that ideal. The following suggestions can help you begin that process in your classroom and eventually in the school building:

◇ **Establish respect rules and do not tolerate anything less.**
When a student complains of being harassed, you need to follow up and determine what happened as soon as possible. Students are more likely to bully if teachers and peers see or are told of their behavior and do nothing to stop it, in effect showing their approval. Tenacity will be the fuel to get the results you want and expect.

◇ **Work together to establish a code of conduct.** Work together as a staff to create a code of conduct for acceptable classroom and schoolwide behaviors. Develop consistent enforcement of effective consequences for verbal and physical aggression that are predictable, immediate, and based on uniform expectations for everyone. Consistent use of logical consequences will reduce bullying and are a necessary part of successful prevention. A discussion of acceptable teacher conduct toward students is beneficial as well. Work out ways that staff can let each other know when a colleague has a momentary lapse into angry or otherwise hurtful behavior.

◇ **Maintain a schoolwide reporting expectation.** While eating lunch in the teachers' cafeteria, I recently overheard one of the cafeteria workers telling the school principal about an incident she had observed several days before between two girls. One student told the other, "You're a slut and everyone knows about it!" When the principal asked the worker why she didn't report it sooner, her reply was, "I was in a hurry and wasn't even sure who to report it to." All staff can report this sort of peer-to-peer aggressive behavior to one central person who is known by everyone. This emphasizes the importance of the behavior and allows quick follow-up.

◇ **Treat all students by the same standard.** It's important that you realize that "good students" can harass. Students have an awareness of what they feel is unfair or discriminatory. Giving favored treatment to so-called "good kids" can be disturbing to others in the class. It's not uncommon that when a student gets labeled as a "troublemaker," we will judge that student far more critically then one we consider a "good student." The reality is that most students misbehave some of the time and all students are aware of who can get away with certain behaviors that others cannot. Respectful schools are possible only if the students respect their teachers, and students lose respect for teachers who appear to engage in stereotyping and discriminatory treatment.

◇ **Respond to hurtful comments and slurs.** Ignorance isn't bliss when students are allowed to use degrading language and hurtful slurs in the classroom. By interrupting degrading comments, you reduce the chance that insults will escalate into threats and violence. You reassure the targeted students that someone cares about their feelings. You also become a model for all students to stand up confidently against harassment.

◇ **Show students that they are important to you.** Many students that identify with admired teachers agree that these teachers are willing to talk to them about what's happening inside and outside of school. To develop a respectful classroom, we need to respect students by valuing their feelings and their lives inside and outside of the classroom. When students feel that their teacher respects and cares about their feelings, they are more likely to feel like they matter in the class and respect their classmates.

◇ **Form listening groups.** Some schools fulfill the need to be listened to by organizing small listening groups, each composed of a teacher advisor and several students who meet regularly to share their concerns and successes. Students look forward to these sessions and often carry on even when the teacher is absent. Besides providing a safe place to vent, listening groups encourage students—and, especially, those potential victims of aggression— to speak up for themselves, to think critically and develop opinions, and to engage more in class.

◇ **Organize a hallway thinking sign(s) campaign.** The purpose of this activity is to teach and remind students in the school about what constitutes a safe and respectful learning community and to provide guidelines on how to become such a school community. You can ask for volunteers to meet and write signs that support respectful, dignified social behavior that reflects the beliefs of your school. These signs can be posted around the school building for all to read and discuss. Following are some examples of Thinking Signs posted in middle and high school hallways:

- Everyone Is Unique

- We Embrace Diversity

- Bullying Is Not Cool!

- Mistakes Are OK. That's How We Learn.

- We Each Learn in Our Own Way, in Our Own Time

- Don't Tolerate Aggressive Behavior

- We Support Random Acts of Kindness

- Weak People Harass Others

- Be a Leader

- It Takes Strength to Be Respectful to Everyone

- If You Can't See the Good in ALL, You Can't See Good at All

- Treat Others As You'd Like Them to Treat You

- Stand Up for Yourself

- Be a Buddy

- Don't Be a Gossip

Pages 62 and 63 show sample Thinking Signs.

BEHAVIORS THAT WILL HELP YOU GET WHAT YOU WANT:

Respecting Others

Following Class Rules

Thinking

Being Helpful

Offering Alternatives

Being Polite

Speaking Up

BEHAVIORS THAT WILL NOT GET YOU WHAT YOU WANT:

Disobeying Rules

Demanding

Disrespecting Others

Blaming Others

Teasing

Gossiping

Harassing Others

Cliques

It is normal for kids to feel left out once in a while. Sometimes friends will argue, separate and later make up again. But it is abnormal and unhealthy for your school community when students form groups that exclude others from belonging. These groups are called *cliques* (pronounced kliks).

What is the difference between a clique and a natural group of like-minded friends? Not all groups of friends are cliques. The difference is that a clique is a group of students that leave out other students *on purpose*. Cliques are led by one or two popular students who are usually bullies and they control who gets to be part of the group. Once part of the clique, it is not unusual for a student to change his or her behavior to conform to the "clique behavior," which is often negative.

For example, Shawn and Bill grew up together and are neighbors. They always socialized together after school. But Jimmy started excluding Bill from the group, and now even Shawn is making fun of Bill. It is the same with Giselle and Amanda. They had invited each other over for sleepovers since second grade. Now Missy is hosting sleepovers, and she doesn't invite Amanda. Giselle has done nothing to change the situation.

Cliques usually form in late elementary school or in middle school. They form around the need to share an intrinsic sense of belonging or popularity and extrinsic interests such as music or sports. Boys and girls both share cliques, though girl cliques tend to be meaner toward the girls who are outside of the group.

Sometimes students in cliques realize that they don't want to belong to it anymore. They don't want to be harassed and bossed around by the leader and rules that govern the clique. They don't feel good about leaving out others and the hurt feelings it creates. They often come to realize that they are missing out on being friends with other good people outside of the clique.

Helping Students Deal with Cliques

Helping students who want to leave a clique and develop more mature and enjoyable friendship groups is essential. Here are some tips to share with students:

◇ **Raise awareness.** Discuss the reasons cliques are formed and how they affect others. Explain that even if someone is not being treated poorly by peers in a clique, that student still might find cliques' unwelcoming attitude annoying. Other students might have come to the point that being part of a clique doesn't feel right anymore and is not worth it. There are things that can be done (see "Offering Opportunities to Make Friends," below, as well as the community-building and school-community-building activities on pages 66–69).

◇ **Speak up.** Advise students not to accept that cliques will happen and are just part of your school community. Tell them to speak up if their group of friends has turned into a clique. It's mature to invite others to be part of their group of friends. The clique might decide to continue without that student, or it may break up and stop acting so exclusive or clique-y.

> **Key Concept**
>
> *Remember: The most popular and well-liked kids are ones who are friendly to everyone.*

◇ **Look for friends.** Advise students to actively make friends with others if they find themselves outside of a clique. A student can do this in a variety of ways, such as joining clubs, saying hello to people he or she may not usually hang out with, acting interested in others because not everyone one meets will be like him or her, inviting someone over to one's house on the weekend even if that student belongs to a clique, and avoiding peers who aren't really friends at all.

Offering Opportunities to Make Friends

We want our students to look for and make friends everywhere and to do their best to let everyone feel welcome to talk with them. Sometimes students who are looking for friends need some structured, supportive activities that offer the opportunity to meet, talk, and play with different peers. Lunchtime is often the only unstructured time for this to occur during school, but it doesn't need to be this way.

Successful gatherings—whether they are called Morning Meetings, Circle of Power, and Respect, or advisory groups—share similar characteristics. We want to provide structured opportunities for all students to get to know each other. Through these activities students can feel welcomed and learn important social skills such as cooperation, communication, empathy, and self-restraint.

Many elementary and middle schools in my district use the Morning Meeting or Circle of Power and Respect for middle schools, a structure developed by Responsive Classroom (www.responsiveclassroom.org). The meeting has four essential components: greeting, sharing group activity, and news and announcements. Students are taught to lead the greeting segment and choose group activities, thus increasing their sense of ownership of the classroom. During the group share, which is very structured but offers an opportunity to discuss topics important to students such as bullying, helping others in need, test anxiety, or a fun party they experienced over the weekend. I have found these meetings to produce more cohesive, cooperative, safe and productive classrooms.

Building Activities

Following are some suggested group-building activities that can be used throughout the week. I have used them successfully at the end and beginning of the day, as well as during a class when I felt students needed a change of pace to refocus their attention and engagement. I've used these activities with elementary, middle, and high school students.

Community-building Activities

⬦ **Coseeki:** Choose one student to leave the room. Then pick a leader, who starts a hand or foot motion that the rest of the students mimic. The first student returns to class and has to determine who the leader is while the leader continually changes the motion without being too obvious.

⬦ **3 Questions and 3 Clues:** Choose a student to wear a card with a category/topic/or name taped on his or her back. They go to the center of a circle and walk around so everyone can read the card. They then must ask three questions and ask three clues to try and guess what's on their card. You can increase the number of questions and clues depending on age of the group.

◇ **2 Truths and 1 Lie:** Ask students to think about two truths about themselves and one lie. Choose one student. Other students then guess what they think is the chosen student's lie. After everyone has a turn to guess the lie, the student reveals his or her answer. Another student then takes a turn.

◇ **Switch It and Change It:** Students form a circle. One student walks inside the circle for a minute so everyone can see what he or she is wearing. After the group examines the student carefully, that student leaves the room and changes one or two things about his or her appearance. The student returns and the group takes turns guessing the change(s). The student that guesses correctly takes the next turn.

◇ **I Spy:** Choose a student to begin this activity. He or she then says, "I spy something _____" (gives an attribute—size, color, shape, "with parallel lines," etc.). Students then make three to five guesses as to what the first student sees. The student who guesses correctly takes the next turn.

◇ **Direct Me:** Ask a student to volunteer to be blindfolded. Place an object somewhere in the room or in the middle of a circle of students. Students then take turns giving directions to the blindfolded student to get him or her to pick up the object. You may want to review good direction techniques before you begin this activity: "Don't say take three steps. Say, 'Turn to your left and take three steps and stop.' "

◇ **Beach Ball Questions:** Devise some questions about information you want to review in class. For example: "Add or subtract the numbers," "What is the square root of this number?", "Define *bully*," "What can you do if someone harasses you?" Write the questions on pieces of masking tape and tape them on different sections of a beach ball. Toss the ball to different students to catch and answer the question closest to their fingers.

School-Community-building Activities

◇ **Promote Community across Grade Levels:** The following activities facilitate friendships between sixth-grade students and older students and therefore reduce the pecking order by grade level. One example of a community-building middle-school activity is "The Amazing Race" scavenger hunt, which brings together sixth, seventh, and eighth graders. You can team each sixth-grade class with a group of seventh and eighth graders to form a "family" that meets at least once a month for this and other community-building activities. Other activities can include, "School Beautification Day" in which students come on a Saturday and work together to plant flowers, collect money through a car wash, organize bulletin boards, and so on.

◇ **Promote Community Service:** Every fall, your school can sponsor a food drive, which introduces them to others in their community who are helping families in need. Each week students can announce at a school meeting or during morning announcements how to many pounds of food have been collected and encourage everyone to keep bringing in cans. When the drive is over, students can learn how to contact the agency responsible for distributing it to people in the community. Both teachers and students can propose service projects, such as raising money to clean up a local park, save the rain forest, or collect toys for children in need during holidays. My summer camp visits a local nursing home and sings uplifting songs to the residents on July 4th.

◇ **Celebrate the Arts and Other Talents:** Find opportunities in your school for students to display art and perform, possibly inspiring other students to consider drawing, painting, poetry, or playing an instrument, singing, or dancing. Other fun activities, such as hand-clapping games, lip-synching performances, class cheers, joke day, and trivia contests, can also act as opportunities to create a feeling of unity and appreciation for each other's talents.

◇ **Create a School Bullying Prevention Committee:** Helping staff understand the importance of modeling respectful behavior for all students is important. When this happens, students are more likely to show respect to peers. A school bullying prevention committee can mentor staff and build staff connections to students. This committee can also arrange staff training, oversee the effectiveness of activities and interventions, suggest any changes, and monitor the consistency of the use of interventions among all staff. The group should be empowered to oversee in a supportive manner. When school staff can expect positive action, they are more likely to be consistent and open to the support they may need.

◇ **Award Peer Intervention:** Without cooperation between students and teachers, bullying can become a big problem that doesn't get better. Too many students do nothing or join in when they see someone being bullied. But the majority of students either try to stop it or want to do something that will be helpful. When students tell a teacher or another adult about a bully, it's a way of saying that bullying is not cool. Part of effective bullying prevention is encouraging students to speak up in safe and responsible ways about bullying, to tell staff what they see and hear, and to befriend isolated peers. Thank students who report aggressive behavior toward themselves and others with a "Leadership Certificate" or "No Bullying Award." Train students who may need and want more effective ways of stopping bullying and exclusion in school.

Building a sense of community is no longer something we can take for granted. We have to build our school communities; affirm the values of non-violence and support for all to succeed, and infuse it with the energy, imagination, and commitment of the entire group. In the practice of being school community members, students find models and pathways that help them move beyond themselves to connect respectfully with others and to make contributions to the greater good. Bullies also need role models for cooperative behavior. Teachers must make it their responsibility to actively create opportunities for this modeling to occur and therefore cultivate the behaviors necessary for a school environment that is free of bullying behavior.

Chapter 3

Helping the Victims

"Cooking someone a meal when they are hungry is good. Teaching them how to cook is best."

*B*eing victimized does not feel good. It stays with you for a long time, possibly your entire life. Protecting students from bullying is part of the solution. Helping them develop the skills necessary for responding to harassment from peers is just as, if not more, important. Your students do not have to live with being bullied by their peers.

Adult Responses to Victims

"I did tell the teacher, Mom! She doesn't care. Billy's always bothering the girls by pulling up their skirts and trying to look down their shirts. Ms. Bell just pretends it's not happening or never sees him doing it." Few parents make it through their children's school years without hearing some comment along these lines. Such complaints may be exaggerated (Billy doesn't *always* harass the girls, or Ms. Bell makes him stop when she *notices*), and it is true that teachers do not always notice bullying even when it happens in their classrooms. Nevertheless, all teachers are aware that bullying occurs.

One of my colleagues once exclaimed, "They're just getting into normal kid conflicts. It's important to let them work it out as long as no one gets hurt." This may be true if it is a "normal kid conflict." But in normal conflicts, both people have some power, which is why these types of normal arguments or conflicts seem to last forever, especially in middle school. When a child is being bullied, there is an obvious imbalance in *power*.

When an imbalance in physical, emotional, intellectual, or social power occurs, you need to intervene as you would with any situation that lacks the balance to resolve itself. For example, if you saw someone drowning, your first reaction would be to quickly intervene as opposed to expecting the drowning person to learn how to swim.

> **Key Concept**
>
> *The bully has the power and the victim has little or none.*

We know that a victim of bullying behavior does not have to remain a victim and that there are many things that can be done to help change the aggressor-victim cycle. Let's first look at this cycle and then examine the problem from students' points of view:

Aggressor–Victim Cycle

Bully harasses victim on playground or in the hallway.

Bully continues to harass victim when adults are not around.

Victim does not tell bully to stop or report incident to adult.

Listen to what students have to say about bullying:

◇ "Kids get made fun of all the time. If you choose to wear something original, the other kids will laugh at you. My friend who has a weight problem walked into class and a boy began mooing while others began laughing. Someone is always watching. It's nerve-wracking."

◇ "The boys snap my bra. The teacher usually ignores it. The teacher keeps teaching and the boys laugh at me."

◇ "I get pushed around by this one kid who thinks he's cool. He knows I won't push back so he comes up to me in the hall or outside and pretends like he's going to hit me. Then he laughs and walks away with his friends. I hate it."

These statements by middle school students reflect an alarming trend in our school communities. Harassment takes on many forms, and victims of abusive behavior are not sure what to do. Most students' responses to harassment include ignoring it, rationalizing it, fighting it, changing their own behavior, or becoming part of a clique to shield themselves from more abuse. Regardless of the defense they choose, all students know that abuse hurts.

Adult responses to allegations of harassment in our schools are inconsistent and consequently may discourage students from further reports, giving them a feeling that they have no place to turn for help. When I've asked students, "Why haven't you reported this to your teacher?", too often their response is "They don't do anything." Other teacher responses students have shared include: "You're overreacting," "I know you're no angel," "What do you expect when you wear clothes like that?", or "Stay away from him and he'll stop."

> ### Key Concept
>
> *Remember: Bullying is not part of growing up, and it destroys self-esteem.*

Although students may exaggerate, the major problem is how they perceive what *does not* happen when they try to get help from adults in their schools. Not all students feel this way, and many do feel that their teachers will respond quickly to end any type of harassment. However, many others hesitate to report abuse or bullying. They remain victims in the shadows of our hallways.

To help break the bully-victim cycle, it's imperative to understand that *all* complaints are important to investigate, and as adult educators, we must be responsive and proactive. We must gain the trust and confidence of all of our students, especially when a problem occurs. Our students need to believe that we will always respond in an assertive manner, even if our initial response is, "That sounds frustrating. I will look into it after lunch."

Identifying Victims

While most students are vulnerable to teasing and general harassment, some students are targeted more than others. The section titled "Who Are the Victims?" in Chapter 1 of this book outlined two types of victims. The students that are being harassed and victimized need to understand the role they are choosing to play. By sharing this information with students as well as adults, you can foster the awareness necessary for the student victim to begin the process of change.

Passive Victims

The passive victim seems to do nothing to invite aggression, and he or she does little or nothing to defend himself or herself when assaulted. Passive victims never do anything to provoke their tormentors and feel unable to stop the bullying behavior therefore rendering themselves helpless. They are non-aggressive and try to avoid confrontation at all costs. They lack self-defense and assertiveness skills. These victims often reward bullies by offering them lunch money, crying, or cowering down to the bullies' demands.

Provocative Victims

The provocative group of victims are usually restless, anxious and hot-tempered. Children with Attention Deficit Hyperactivity Disorder (ADHD) can fall into this category. They tend to have poor impulse control and interpersonal skills. The fact that they do not "fit in" sets them up to be victimized by others. Not all provocative victims exhibit anxious and hot-tempered behavior but they do tend to tease and taunt the bullies.

As you can see, students become victims for so many reasons that it is foolish to make stereotyped assumptions about any child's experience. These "victim patterns" seem to begin with low self-esteem and a lack of adult intervention. We know that girls are teased more for the way they look and boys for the way they act. Harassment and bullying of boys often take the form of homophobic insults, in which boys are called *gay, old lady, girl,* or other names linked to feminine behavior. By looking past the stereotypes of the root causes of victim-like behavior, you will be in a much better position to help your students and their families.

Stopping harassment and bullying requires changing the abusive culture that a school can inhabit. Protecting victims begins with identifying them with *objective* observation. Then mindful interventions can begin.

Identifying Victims Checklist

There are many warning signs that point to a student who may be being victimized in school or at home. The following checklist can help identify victims or potential victims in your school.

Student's name: _____ Date: _____

Teacher filling out checklist: _____

School Observations

_____ Sits by him or herself

_____ Seldom initiates a conversation

_____ Seems chronically bored with school

_____ Avoids eye contact, has poor posture, looks at the ground when walking

_____ Has poor attendance

_____ Clings to teacher

_____ Lack of interest in school-sponsored activities

_____ Low academic achievement

Social-Emotional Behavior

_____ Avoids students in social situations

_____ Seems irritable and uncomfortable in school

_____ May exhibit impulsive and hyperactive behavior

_____ Passive responses to direct questions from adults and peers

_____ Usually does not eat lunch

_____ Nervous, fearful, insecure

_____ Talks a lot about personal safety in school, on bus, walking home

_____ Avoids certain places in building, such as lockers during gym, the bathroom, and so on

_____ Talks about hurting him- or herself

_____ Is always on the verge of crying about minor incidents

_____ Has been caught carrying a weapon to school

A Special Case: Victims of Sexual Bullying

Most bullying and harassment is focused on verbal abuse. In many middle and high schools, this behavior is pervasive—particularly sexual harassment. Abusive teasing among peers seems to be the norm. Many students say that harassment is a way of life: "Kids make fun of you. The way you dress, your hair, how you talk. They're just mean."

All schools have policies against sexual harassment, but how well are they explained and enforced by staff? I was walking down the hallway of a middle school and overheard a young boy tell a girl walking by him that she needed to get liposuction. The girl kept walking and I stopped the boy and asked, "Why would you say such a hurtful thing to her?" His response was, "She always bothers me and she's loose anyway." Studies also indicate that sexually active girls are not the only ones who are labeled with such words as *loose, slut*, or *whore*. Any girl who demonstrates vulnerability may be harassed in this way.

Victims of sexual bullying may exhibit any or all of the following behaviors:

- Eating disorders, such as bulimia or anorexia

- Excessive bathing or poor hygiene

- Withdrawal from family members

- Sexual activity at an early age

- Regression to childlike behaviors

All bullying deprives children of their self-esteem and confidence, but for obvious reasons sexual harassment and abuse can lead to the most extreme emotional consequences. When trying to determine if a student has been sexually labeled, harassed, or abused, take extra care to protect the student's privacy and well-being.

Finding Support

When you think you've identified a student who may be a victim or is at risk of being bullied, it's important that you share your concerns with other staff.

- ◇ Talk with other teachers about your observations and concerns.

- ◇ Get information from the physical education staff. (Remember that bullying is more prevalent in places with little or no supervision, such as locker rooms, so p.e. teachers may have had to address incidents of bullying in their classes.)

◇ Share the "Identifying Victims Checklist" with other school faculty.

◇ Notify the school nurse if warning signs such as frequent illness, stomachaches, or headaches frequently occur. The nurse can question the student privately to see if these symptoms have other causes, such as being harassed or bullied.

Talking to other teachers and staff can help you determine if the warning signs you've observed are isolated incidents or not. If you find that they are isolated incidents, then more investigation may be needed to determine its causes.

Most schools have a counselor whose responsibility is to meet with students who may be having behavior problems or who need support with external problems that are affecting their schoolwork, such as parents divorcing, their pet having just died, or conflicts with friends. (In my school district we call these helpers *adjustment counselors*.)

Students who are having these problems or are sick of being bullied by someone else in their school need a person with whom to share their feelings and thoughts. Sometimes the school counselor may be just that person. They should be aware of this opportunity and what the counselor can and cannot do for them. You can use this list to help explain to students how the school counselor can help them:

◇ They know how to listen and can help with life's challenges.

◇ Counselors have special training in how to solve problems, make decisions, and help you to stand up for yourself.

◇ They will not wave a magic wand to make the problem go away, but they will help you cope with it.

◇ Coping means that someone is trying to handle a problem such as bullying and make things better.

◇ They will take your problem seriously and help you find a solution.

◇ The counselor wants to help you to learn to be a contributing member of the school community without fear or insecurity.

◇ Counselors generally meet students in a private meeting, group meetings with other peers, or in classrooms, where they teach a class on a subject such as bullying.

You can explain to your students that if someone is bullying them, the counselor will talk to them about it and can give them some ideas and strategies on how to deal with the bully. The counselor may also talk to the bully and other peers who saw what happened. The counselor may also get additional information and support by talking to other teachers and parents about the problem. Let students know that this may feel a little uncomfortable, facing the problem but trying to correct it is better than living with a bad situation. Getting a counselor's help means students do not have to face difficult school problems alone.

John F. Kennedy Middle School adjustment counselor Tim Murphy often tells fables, stories, or uses storybooks to help reach and teach students. *Loudmouth George and the Sixth-Grade Bully* by Nancy Carlson is one of the resources he uses when discussing bullying. He first asks students to look at the book's illustrations or the characters' "non-verbal communication." One of the key words he focuses on when counseling is *empathy* or walking in the shoes of a victim or bully. Discussion then leads to why one may become a bully or victim. Tim Murphy points out that Loudmouth George (a rabbit) is innocently walking to school with his backpack on and carrying his lunch and, like most kids, he wants to get an education and feel safe. He points out the predator-prey relationship that is part of the animal world is synonymous to the bully-victim relationship for people. The first act of harassment occurs when Big Mike (a bear bully) says to George, "Hi-ya, squirt. Gimme all your money or I won't let you by." The story goes on to illustrate how George begins to lose his ability to concentrate in class while feeling very insecure about walking home.

Tim Murphy doesn't finish the book with his students because at the end George decides to retaliate. Murphy doesn't think that retaliation is an effective response for students to consider. Instead he brainstorms other responses to being bullied, including asking responsible adults for help. He then connects with the student during the week to see how things are progressing.

School counselors can meet with a student privately, visit a class, or talk at a school assembly to let students know they are available. It's a good idea to let everyone know about the school counselor, even if a problem is not immediately apparent.

For Teachers: Helping Families of Victims

All over the country, school and community people are coming together to help schools meet the varied needs of today's students and their parents. To better serve families, some school systems have formed partnerships with outside agencies—public mental health, social services, police, and drug and alcohol agencies, as well as nonprofit support agencies. Schools are embracing support from any source that can be of help.

For example, two fathers and their sons visited a Parent Center to discuss an incident that had occurred between the two boys. This discussion, which began at school with the principal and counselor, soon became a conversation between the two fathers on the challenges of managing their boy's behaviors, one being a bully and the other a victim. It ended with one father giving some advice to the other father, advice that was appreciatively received. Many times, bringing parents together is not a good idea, especially if each parent is avoiding any responsibility for their child's aggressive behavior toward others. In this case, while some problems in a school may be addressed by social workers or school psychologists, other solutions may just as easily be found among the network of caring individuals, whether it's a teacher, paraprofessional, or parent.

Bullying at Home

While it is true that most bullying takes place on school grounds, it can occur in any unsupervised location, such as in one's home. Here's one student's story: "My big brother tortured me practically from birth. He'd always scare me, push me around when I got on his nerves. My parents never believed me when I tried to tell them how he was. I couldn't wait to get out of the house." In this case, this student's parents may have been effective in protecting her from bullying in the neighborhood, but they had clearly never considered their own home as a possible setting for abusive behavior.

Research has shown us that creating not only a school but ideally a home environment that can be characterized by the following principles will support safe and secure environments for all students. Share these principles with families whose children are at risk of being bullied or being a bully:

◇ Develop a supportive and caring environment; show interest in your children's lives.

◇ Establish firm limits on unacceptable behavior.

◇ Consistent use of non-punitive, nonphysical sanctions for unacceptable behavior

◇ Be an adult who acts as a positive role model for effective communication by listening to your children and expressing your anger without blaming or hurting others.

Parents as well as teachers and students play major roles in carrying out an anti-bullying program. It's important that parents are made aware of the information provided in this book about what a victim is and how you can help parents deal with this problem. Parents should also understand that a school climate of fear can affect more that just the students that are victims.

We know that bullying often occurs away from adults, but most students often witness bullying events. As bystanders, they are confused about what to do and may fear becoming the next target. Parents can take an active role at home in creating and implementing prevention techniques. Following are some techniques that can effectively support positive change. First, offer parents the "Help Us Create a School Free of Bullying" handout (p. 80). Make up a handout with questions they can consider asking when talking to their child. It is just as important for their child to recognize when bullying is taking place and how to differentiate it from "just kidding around" behavior.

Help Us Create a School Free of Bullying

Dear Parents,

We are committed to creating and maintaining a school community that has caring educators and involved parents and is safe, respectful, and free of bullying. The following information will help you understand how you can help us in our efforts to build a partnership between school and home for the purpose of meeting our safe school goals.

What Is Bullying?

◇ Bullying occurs when a person is repeatedly mean and hurtful toward someone else, often when that person has trouble defending himself or herself.

◇ The bully gets satisfaction when he or she gets a reaction out of the person being bullied, the victim.

What Your Child Can Do When Being Bullied

◇ Do not keep it a secret from the people around you.

◇ Tell adults when bullying is happening to them, a friend, or classmate.

What Should Parents Do?

◇ Adults should take action to prevent bullying and discipline students who are bullies.

◇ Talk to your children about bullying behavior and ask them if they have either witnessed it or have been bullied at school or on the bus. You can use the "Questions to Ask" handout as a guide for suggested questions to ask your child.

◇ Let your child know that they will be helped and will never get in trouble for sharing their experiences about bullying and harassment at school.

◇ Notify the school principal and ask to meet with any staff that would be able to help deal with the problem at hand as soon as possible.

◇ Remember, the best way to help your child during this anxious time is to work cooperatively with the teachers and administrators at school.

Sincerely,

Getting Information from Parents

When talking to parents about their child's problem at school, it's important to begin with a message of support and the school's commitment to creating and maintaining an environment that is free of bullying behavior. Next you may want to tell the parent that you've noticed behaviors from their child that may indicate that they may be a victim of being bullied. Parents' knowledge of their child's behavior at home may indicate other warning signs that don't show up during school. When discussing the possibility of a child being a victim of bullying, it's important to look beyond surface appearances to the real elements that determine which child a bully will target. Help parents understand that the essential quality any bully will look for in a victim is not difference but *vulnerability*. A bully wants to abuse without the concern of retaliation. For example, if the student wears unfashionable clothes but has good social skills that include making and having friends, he or she is particularly not vulnerable to being victimized. (Friends will most likely defend him or her from the bully.) If the student is somewhat isolated and withdrawn, then regardless of age, physical appearance, race, religion, or socioeconomic status, he or she is more vulnerable.

> **Key Concept**
>
> *Shyness, a lack of friends, and absence of adult support will make a student an especially likely target.*

While it is difficult for any parent to see his or her child in an objective light—especially as that child appears to teachers and peers—assessing the child's social skills and behaviors is a vital first step in protecting them from being bullied. Ask a parent questions that will give you more insight into the student, such as:

- Seems moody, anxious, depressed, and refuses to discuss how school is going

- Wants to stay home for minor illnesses or is reluctant to go to school

- Resistant to taking the bus, walking home, or taking the same walking route to school

- Comes home hungry (possibly, bullies have stolen lunch money)

- Experiences bed-wetting, nightmares, or difficulty sleeping

- Waits to get home to use the bathroom

- Experiences frequent crying or uncommon emotional outbursts

- Frequently comes home with bruises or ripped clothing or has lost belongings

- Rarely talks to or socializes with peers

- Found carrying a weapon for "protection"

- Talks about wanting to get stronger or take a martial art

- Talks about wanting to hurt others and him- or herself

Additional Questions for Parents

◇ Do you have any concern that your child is having problems with other children at school?

◇ Does your child go to the school nurse frequently?

◇ Do you suspect that your child is being harassed or bullied at school or in the neighborhood for any reason? If so, why?

While discussing these behaviors, share with parents any other behaviors that may indicate that their child is being bullied and/or harassed at school, at home or in the neighborhood. If the student exhibits any of these symptoms, he or she is at risk of being victimized and needs help. Let the parents know that you are committed to helping their child feel safe and secure at school and that you'll communicate with them as often as necessary to stop any bullying behavior. Offer your assistance by suggesting that a parent-teacher conference be scheduled as soon as possible to deal with this issue. You may find it helpful to invite the student to participate in the conference from the start; some teachers would rather have the student wait until the parent and other concerned adults discuss the matter.

How to Interview a Victim

Part of the process of helping the family of a bullying victim is interviewing the student. This can be a delicate situation. Here are some tips for setting up and carrying out an interview with a student whom you suspect is being bullied.

First and foremost, it's important to arrange to do the interview in a room where you'll have privacy without interruptions. Children who are bullied may perceive their world as a threatening, unsafe place and become suspicious and withdrawn.

When interviewing a student, your role is not one of judge and jury but a nonjudgmental facilitator who encourages open communication and problem solving, which may include suggesting alternate behaviors (refer to "Changing Bad Feelings," p. 93). Following are some sample questions to ask during the interview:

- Did the student hurt you on purpose?

- Did this behavior happen more than one time?

- How did it make you feel?

- Did the student know that he or she was hurting you?

- Did you hurt her or him first?

- What did she or he say to you while this happened?

- What would you like to happen?

It's also very important to be a good listener. Practice the following tips to cultivate your active listening skills:

◇ **Look at the speaker.** Eye contact and silence require concentration.

◇ **Ask questions.** For example, "What where you doing when she said that?"

◇ **Repeat what the speaker is saying.** For example, "It sounds like you got really upset when Jason kept pointing his finger at you."

◇ **Don't interrupt.** Allow time for the speaker to finish his or her thoughts. Refrain from problem solving for the speaker.

◇ **Keep conversation going.** One technique for doing this is using brief interjections to show you are really listening—for example, "Yes," "I see," "Uh-huh," "Really," "So then what happened?"

The interview should take no longer than ten minutes. If you decide to interview the bully, determine first if there are others involved and how long it has been going on. Do the initial interview separately and then bring the victim and bully together. When conducting two or more interviews, schedule them so there is no time in between for the students involved to talk to each other.

Within a reasonable amount of time (two to three days), have a follow-up meeting to determine if the agreed-upon changes occurred. If they did, encourage the students to continue and praise their maturity. If the agreed-upon changes have not occurred, then you need to objectively analyze the next step needs. After a discussion as to why the behaviors have not stopped, you may find that students need more time to implement the follow-up plan.

The bully and victim may need to complete the activities in this book as a skills and awareness training class. You may also consider referring the student bully for a comprehensive evaluation by a trained mental health professional.

The following scenarios are sample interviews that you can use as a guide for your discussion with someone whom you suspect might be a victim of bullying.

Passive Victim:

Adult: Sharon, can we sit and talk about something that I've been wanting to discuss with you?

Student: Yea, I guess so.

Adult: Good. Let's meet next period.

Adult: I've noticed some other students bothering you during lunch.

Student: They're jerks. They just want to make fun of me, my hair and the way I talk. I don't care about them.

Adult: You don't care about how they treat you?

Student: I wish they would just leave me alone.

Adult: What do you think can happen that might help the situation?

Student: I could stop coming to school or maybe eat lunch with you in class.

Adult: You think staying home or staying away from the lunch room would solve the problem?

Student: My parents wouldn't let me stay home but maybe you would let me eat lunch with you.

Adult: Is there any student that you like sitting with?

Student: Yeah, Kim but she has to sit with her class. The other kids usually don't say anything to me when Kim's around.

Adult: If I talk with Kim's teacher, maybe she would let you sit with her class and Kim. Do you want me to ask Mrs. Hall?

Student: I guess so.

Adult: Okay. I'll let you know what Mrs. Hall says tomorrow morning and we'll see how it goes.

Provocative Victim:

Adult: John, can we sit and talk about something that I've been wanting to discuss with you?

Student: If you're talking about George, I'm not afraid of him.

Adult: Okay. Let's sit down after lunch.

Adult (later)**:** So, you're not afraid of George.

Student: Yeah. He thinks he's so smart. I'm tired of him threatening to hurt me if I don't stop.

Adult: What does he want you to stop doing?

Student: I just joke around with him. I like telling him he looks like King Kong and he gets all bent out of shape. He just can't take a joke.

Adult: George doesn't like being called King Kong.

Student: It's just a joke. Then he and his friends push me around outside and take my stuff. That really gets me mad.

Adult: Pushing you around and taking your belongings is not right either. What do you think can happen that might help the situation?

Student: I can start taking their stuff.

Adult: You really think that would stop them from bothering you?

Student: Maybe I should leave him alone or stop calling him King Kong.

Adult: That sounds like a good place to start. Let's talk in a few days and see how it works.

For Parents: Helping Your Child Deal with Bullying

How to Talk to Your Child about Bullying

1. Show interest. Children, and especially teenagers, are quick to note when an adult is not interested in what they have to say or in helping them, and victims of bullying feel especially vulnerable to judgment. By asking specific questions versus "How was your day at school?", you are more likely to get a response from your child. Don't isolate your child even more by not taking the time to hear what he or she might have to say. First concentrate on the kinds of things that have been happening rather than particular incidents. Spend some uninterrupted time asking your child questions such as these:

Questions for Younger Children:

- Have you ever been unhappy at school?

- Does anyone ever bother you at school?

- I noticed your shirt is ripped. How did it happen? Did someone do that to you?

- Do you know what a bully is? Who's the bully in your school?

- At recess, do you play with other children or by yourself?

- Do you ever get into fights at school? Does the bully ever pick on you?

- Has anyone ever touched you in a way you don't like? Where and how?

- Do other kids ever tease you or make fun of you because of how you act or who you are? What do they say?

- Is there anyone in your class that you wished wasn't there? Why?

- Does anyone bother you or anyone else on the school bus? What do they do?

Questions for Older Children:

- You seem to want to stay home a lot. Is there something happening at school or anywhere else that's making you feel this way?

- Sometimes I get so mad I feel like hitting somebody. Do you ever feel that way?

- Who are your friends? Who would you go to a movie with them or have someone over to the house?

- Are there a lot of cliques in your school? What do you think of them?

- What do other kids say about the clothes you wear?

- Anyone tease you about the way you look? Your body?

- How do you deal with being teased?

- Do you feel your clothes fit in at school? Do others dress like you? Like who?

- Has anyone ever tried to touch you in an inappropriate way without your permission?

These types of questions will usually lead to emotional confidence from your child. If your child tells you that she or he is being harassed by someone at school or in the neighborhood, support their feelings by believing them. Get as much information as they will comfortably tell you. Avoid saying what you will or will not do other than that you will help them deal with this difficult situation. It's best to say that the bullies will not get in trouble but will get help to stop what they are doing. Without this assurance, your child may be reluctant to give any names. Remember, being bullied is never the victim's fault.

2. Take action. Once you and your child have determined that bullying is occurring, it is time to decided together what action needs to take place. Take children's complaints of bullying seriously. The bottom line for all such conversations must be that if your child feels that he or she is in physical danger, he or she cannot handle the situation alone. Adults must intervene. Contacting the teacher, principal, counselor, or anyone else you feel comfortable discussing this with at school is the next step.

Share with the school what you discussed with your child. Request a meeting to decide what action needs to take place in order to ensure that your child feels safe at school. Bring a written record of what your child shared with you. Developing a partnership between you and the school's staff will help you monitor your child's safety at school. Be open to feedback and suggestions from your child's teacher. By working as a team, everyone can help diminish the emotional impact of the bullying incident while strengthening the bond between all the helpers involved. Everyone wants to help find long-term solutions to this problem.

The purpose of meeting with school staff is to reassure the victim that the problem can be solved and to find out:

- Who are the main threatening figures, the "bullies"

- Who are present although may not actively join in the bullying, the "bystanders"

- Who may be the victim's supporters or who he or she would like to have as friends

3. Teach and practice assertive responses. Sometimes the best way to stop a bully is a clear, assertive statement that the bully's behavior is not welcome or appreciated. Passive responses (looking away, meekly smiling or looking confused, not saying anything, etc.) usually provokes more harassment. Aggressive responses (returning an insult, threatening the bully, etc.) may lead to an escalation of harassment and violence. Rational questions or comments that directly address the conflict may stop the bully from continuing.
Your child may benefit from both of you practicing the following assertive statements before his or her next encounter with a bully. Explain to your child that both of you are going to rehearse some responses to another student's negative comments. One person takes the role of the bully, and the other the assertive student.

Bully: You're a real idiot.

Response: Why would you say that?

Bully: You're a fag.

Response: What makes you think I'm like that?

Bully: If you keep saying that, I'm gonna make you hurt!

Response: If we don't agree on something, can we just talk about it reasonably or better yet just drop it?

Bully: Hey, there's the teacher's pet.

Response: I'm sorry you feel that way, but it's not true.

Helping your child deal directly with abusive comments such as these is the first supportive step in enhancing how they feel about themselves. Once your child has interacted with the bully and has reported the results, discuss how effective his or her response turned out to be. If the abusive comments continue, then discuss the need for another action which may involve talking to the school teachers and principal.

Tips for Reducing Bullying:

◇ Listen to your child. Get him or her to admit there is a problem.

◇ Help your child search for answers. Express confidence that the problem can be solved. Don't expect him or her to work it out alone.

◇ Make it clear that it is not his or her fault.

◇ Teach self-respect. Help your child develop a sense of his or her own personal power by assertively communicate needs.

◇ Encourage your child to seek help from an adult at school.

◇ Emphasize that there is no shame in asking for help but that it takes maturity and inner strength.

◇ Recommend walking away from verbal insults.

◇ Do not teach or tell your child to fight back.

◇ Encourage friendships.

◇ Find established social skills classes that he or she can participate in.

◇ Intervene and show your child bullying is not tolerated.

◇ Get involved in the school. Become a parent-partner to eliminate bullying from school. Work with other parents to ensure that the neighborhood children are supervised closely on their way to and from school.

When Your Child Is a Bystander

Students who watch bullying often tend to identify with the bully, not the victim, and may even cheer on the abuse! Even if other students in the school do not cheer on the bully, the fact that they just stand and watch sends a message to the bully that lets the abuse continue.

> **Key Concept**
>
> *Fortunately, if someone does intervene, bullying usually stops quickly.*

Once a parent and child have agreed that witnessing a bullying incident and doing nothing is rarely acceptable, she or he will need to know what can be done to help the victim. When your child has witnessed a specific bullying incident and is concerned about whether or not to intervene, you will need to walk him or her through the scenario to decide what the best options are. Ask your child to describe the bully to you—size and strength, level of popularity, history of bullying, and any history of getting in trouble at school. If your child is at least as popular, she or he may be able to discourage the bully with a distracting comment or action such as: "Come on, Tom, pick on someone your own age. Let's go."

You may also want to know about other witnesses to the incident. Will these other students back your child if he or she needs help? You and your child need to also discuss the reliability of adult support where bullying is taking place. If your child's school has an active anti-bullying program, it is among the easiest places for a bystander to intervene successfully. A school where "the teachers rarely listen or do anything to stop Tom from bothering others" is a higher-risk place to intervene because your child may not get the backup protection after she or he has intervened.

What Not to Do as a Bystander

- Directly interfere if you are alone

- Attempt to fight the bully physically

- Walk away without reporting the incident or asking for help

What to Do as a Bystander

◇ **Point out the problem.** Sometimes just letting the bully know what's happening can be enough to stop a bullying action before it gets more momentum. For example, "We're not supposed to hit," "That's sexual harassment," "You're not supposed to pick on the younger kids," "She is perfectly fine just the way she is," "Just because he's different doesn't mean you should be picking on him."

◇ **Tell a teacher.** Some students do not have the emotional or social strength and skills to stop bullying on their own. In these cases your child needs to feel comfortable calling on adults for help. Talk with your child about whom he or she might ask for help in the classroom, on the playground, on the school bus, and in the neighborhood.

◇ **Help the victim.** Whether or not your child can intervene for the purposes of stopping a bullying incident, he or she may be able to help the victim in private later on. Becoming friends may be what is needed to bolster the victim's self-confidence. Supporting the victim's ability to ask an adult for help can be what is needed to stop the bully-victim cycle from continuing.

◇ **Help the bully.** If your child knows the bully, he or she may be able to talk to him about changing his bullying behavior. Reminding a bully about the trouble he or she can get into if it continues can be effective. A simple "Let him alone. He's okay" can sometimes work if your child has sufficient social status among the group. If the bully persists in harassing others, you child will have to consider how to report the incident to a responsible adult before the situation gets worse.

Tips for Empowering Your Child

The following suggestions do not require a lot of effort but can make a big difference. You can boost your child's confidence and self-esteem by:

◇ Talking about his or her strengths, ideas, and dreams.

◇ Reminding him or her on a frequent basis that she or he is loved and valued through conversations at bedtime, notes in lunchboxes, and so on.

◇ Asking for his or her opinions when dealing with day-to-day issues at home.

◇ Display artwork or graded schoolwork prominently, letting your child know his or her work is appreciated and creative. (Refrigerators make great art galleries!)

◇ Creating opportunities to be helpful and complimenting him or her on a job well done.

◇ Your child may feel stressed by a situation occurring at school. Be aware to ease up on your pressure for him or her to perform. Make leeway for mistakes.

◇ Be honest.

◇ Involve your child in problem-solving and decision-making relative to his or her own life. Respect his or her feelings, needs, wants, and suggestions.

◇ Be a good model—think well of yourself, be assertive, and stand up for yourself.

◇ Read stories about bullying and self-esteem (see the Resources section on p. 174).

◇ Even though your child may need your guidance and advice, avoid being judgmental, giving lots of "shoulds." One student once said to me, "My parents are always telling me that I should do this and should do that. I'm feeling 'should on'!"

Changing Bad Feelings

If your child expresses negative self-feelings, be careful not to contradict the child. For example, if he or she says, "I don't have any friends," one may be tempted to say, "Oh, that's not true! You're liked by a lot of kids your age." To do this would only serve to increase the bad feelings, not to change them. The change must come from within your child, and this can only happen by allowing and accepting his or her bad feelings.

Once your child communicates bad feelings openly, then they can be fully explored and talked about. The following example of a parent and child dialogue may be helpful in understanding how to proceed from this point:

Child: I don't have any real friends. Other kids don't want to be with me.

Parent: There aren't any kids who like you at school or in our family?

Child: Well only one kid at school, Terry, will talk to me and my cousin Sam.

Parent: So two kids your age are friendly to you.

Child: Yeah. We like doing things together. But other kids either bother me or ignore me and I try to be their friend.

The child's response is a good example of a theory of change that states: *Change occurs when one becomes what he is, not when he tries to become what he is not.* This conversation can then move into what sort of things happen when other children ignore him and why he thinks Terry and Sam are friendly to him.

As parents, we want to resist the temptation for solving all of our children's problems. This theory asks us to stop trying to be the change agent for our children, and by doing so we make meaningful and orderly change possible.

To help a child who is being victimized to feel better, we need to bring him or her back to himself. The first and essential step in this process is to accept his or her present feelings regardless of how bad they may seem. As the *child* accepts these feelings, he or she can become reacquainted with his or her positive qualities and learn about himself or herself from the inside, instead of through judgments and opinions of others. The child can also begin to feel that it is possible to change how he or she thinks, and therefore change how he or she feels.

Empowering Interventions

Teach your students, especially those who are prone to being victims of harassment or bullying, how to assert themselves, thereby empowering them. The following activities do just that. These activities can be done with the whole class, a small group, or an individual student.

Speak Up for Yourself

Sometimes students find it difficult to speak up for themselves. Instead a student may let people walk all over him or her. Becoming a "human doormat" is a choice one does not have to make. Instead, a student can learn to be assertive and therefore handle situations in a way that puts him or her in control.

To begin, hand out page 95. Have students read and study the list of verbal and nonverbal assertive skills. Then have students pair up and quiz each other. When they're ready, have them take the written quiz. Afterward, hold a class discussion.

Name _____   Date _____

Speak Up for Yourself

Directions: Read and study the following Verbal and Nonverbal Assertive Skills. Then with a partner, quiz each other. When you're ready, take the quiz below.

Verbal and Nonverbal Assertive Skills

1. **Voice Volume:** Speak with a strong confident tone of voice.
   For example: "I don't want to give you my money so stop asking me."

2. **Smooth Talk:** Speak in a smooth way without hesitating or repeating your words. *For example*: "Excuse me, I need to go to class" versus "Can I, umm, can you move, I . . ."

3. **Eye Contact:** Look into the eyes of the person to whom you are talking.

4. **Body Posture:** Stand tall and straight. Face the person to whom you are talking.

5. **Distance:** Stand at a respectful distance, about 3 feet away from the person.

Directions: Now, in your own words, write the definitions of these behaviors. Then check your answers with the correct definitions.

1. **Voice Volume:** _____

   _____

2. **Smooth Talk:** _____

   _____

3. **Eye Contact:** _____

   _____

4. **Body Posture:** _____

   _____

5. **Distance:** _____

   _____

Practice Being Assertive

Hand out copies of page 97. Allow students time to read and respond to each situation. Following are some possible responses:

1. "I don't want to make fun of her. What did she ever do to you?" "I don't like making fun of other kids." "I wouldn't want someone to make fun of me if I was new." "Why do you want to make fun of him? I don't think that is right."

2. Ignore him. "That's your opinion." "No, I'm not." "Why would you say something like that to me?" "I don't like being called names."

3. "I can't concentrate on my work because I'm being harassed." "I need you to help me by doing something about this." "Can I have a pass to talk to the principal?"

As follow-ups, have students try role-playing being assertive. This allows them time to practice the skills necessary to feel more confident and therefore be assertive in a real-life situation. Ask for volunteers to take turns standing in front of the class and role-play a scenario using their responses.

Express Yourself

Before handing out the copies of pp. 98 and 99, explain to students that to act assertively, they must know at least two things about themselves:

1. Their feelings

2. What they want

Write these on the chalkboard or newsprint. Then read them out loud. Next give each student the handout. Read the example out loud and check for understanding. When you think everyone understands the steps for communicating assertively, ask them to fill out the sheet. Review and discuss answers individually and/or as a group.

Name _____ Date _____

Practice Being Assertive

Directions: Read each situation and write down how you would respond assertively without trying to hurt the other person's feelings. Next compare your answers with a partner and share with the class.

1. **Situation:** A friend wants you to make fun of a new student who recently came to your school. The new student dresses differently than most of the students in your school.

   What would you say? _____

   _____

2. **Situation:** A student who tends to bother others looks at you and calls you a wimp.

   What would you say? _____

   _____

3. **Situation:** You tell your teacher that another student is always bothering you. Your teacher says to just ignore it and concentrate on your classwork.

   What would you say? _____

   _____

Express Yourself

Example:

Situation: Andrew is told by his friend to walk behind Eric and grab his arms while standing behind him. Eric is shy and doesn't like to be touched. He pushes Andrew away and calls him a name. Andrew pushes him back and the teacher walks into class. When questioned, Andrew says he was just fooling around and Eric went "crazy."

What could Eric say to Andrew?

• **I feel** <u>confused and angry</u>

• **when you** <u>stand behind me and grab my arms.</u>

• **I want** <u>you to not touch me unless I say it's okay.</u>

Directions: Read the following situations. Then answer the questions below each.

Situation: Crystal writes a note to her friend that makes fun of the way Karen is dressed. Karen is told about the note from another student who is her friend.

What could Karen say to Crystal?

• **I feel** _____

• **when you** _____

• **I want** _____

Situation: Sam calls Robbie a queer and tells him to hide in a closet.

What could Robbie say to Sam?

• **I feel** _____

• **when you** _____

• **I want** _____

Name _____   Date _____

Express Yourself (continued)

Situation: Alfonzo tells Nate that after school he better watch his back.

What could Nate say to Alfonzo?

- **I feel** _____

- **when you** _____

- **I want** _____

Situation: Melinda calls Shanti teacher's pet. Some students who overheard Melinda's comment begin to laugh. Melinda smiles and stares at Shanti.

What could Shanti say to Melinda?

- **I feel** _____

- **when you** _____

- **I want** _____

Situation: Marcos is told by the class bully that he should go on a diet before he blows up.

What could Marcos say to the class bully?

- **I feel** _____

- **when you** _____

- **I want** _____

Now try writing a situation on your own.

Situation: _____

_____

What could _____ *say to* _____?

- **I feel** _____

- **when you** _____

- **I want** _____

Violence and Peace

Most of us have five senses: sight, hearing, touching, taste, and smell. This activity asks students to call on some of these senses by completing the sentences on page 101 *without* thinking too much about the answers. After everyone has completed their sentences, ask for volunteers to read their answers out loud as you list them on the chalkboard or on newsprint. Then ask the group these questions:

- What do you notice about these lists?

- What are similar? Different?

Discuss the answers as a class.

Possible Solutions to Difficult Situations

Students can do this activity individually, in pairs, or in a group. First, hand out copies of page 102. Have students read about each situation on the sheet and then read the list of solutions below. Ask students to match each situation with a possible solution. When everyone has finished the activity, hold a class discussion, asking students to answer the following questions:

- Were some of the solutions more realistic than others? Why?

- What are some other solutions you could add to the list?

Note that you can make new worksheets for this activity by adapting the lists of situations and solutions to your own student's needs. Take time to add as many other appropriate possible solutions and situations necessary to include what may be happening in your class or school.

Name _____   Date _____

Violence and Peace

Directions: Complete the sentences below with the first thing that comes to mind for each question.

What does Violence:

Look like? _____

_____

_____

Sound Like? _____

_____

_____

Feel Like? _____

_____

_____

What does Peace:

Look like? _____

_____

_____

Sound Like? _____

_____

_____

Feel Like? _____

_____

_____

Name _____   Date _____

Possible Solutions to Difficult Situations

Directions: Match a possible assertive solution to each difficult situation listed below.

Difficult Situations

1. A student threatens to beat you up after school.

2. Someone that has picked on you throws a piece of food at you in the cafeteria.

3. A group of peers surrounds you and starts calling you names.

4. You notice an older student harassing a younger friend in the hallway.

5. The vice principal says you are being watched, so you better watch your step.

6. Someone shoulders you when passing in the hall.

7. A bigger student demands that you give him your lunch money.

8. Your peers try to get you to trip another student on the playground.

Possible Solutions

_____ I don't need to get into any more trouble. I can avoid trouble by staying out of it.

_____ Talk it out with an adult you can trust.

_____ Find a teacher as soon as possible and report the incident.

_____ Tell yourself: "I don't want to get into a fight. I need to get some advice."

_____ Tell yourself: "I don't need to get angry or blow up right now. I'll keep going."

_____ Tell yourself: "I don't want to hurt anyone." Then express yourself to your peers.

_____ If you feel safe, assert yourself by saying: "That's harassment and it's not right."

_____ If you feel safe, assert yourself by saying: "Sorry I don't have anything to give you." Tell an adult about the difficult situation.

Chapter 4

Helping the Bullies

"Teaching some children is like looking for gold. You have to get past a lot of dirt before getting to the good stuff."

Student diversity is one of the great strengths of our public schools. Students with different learning strengths and weaknesses, students from various cultures, and students with physical challenges all bring special gifts that can enrich our school communities. But what about working with the aggressive student who bullies others? These students can present a daunting challenge to any educator.

Adult Responses to Bullies

One perspective in working with student bullies is that they are behaving in a manner that stops them from becoming full participants in their school community, therefore putting us all at risk. Many teachers hesitate to initiate discussions with bullies because they fear that making issues of bullying behavior may make it worse. They hope that by ignoring it that somehow the problem will go away—or they fear that they lack the skills or classroom norms for such a discussion. These concerns are genuine.

Other adults fall into the behavior paradox of becoming aggressive with the aggressor or "bullying the bully." Threatening, blaming, and intimidating may achieve temporary gains but long-term losses. If the issue of *effectively* helping the bully to stop being an aggressor is not dealt with, we all lose our ability to provide a safe and uplifting school environment for all our children and staff.

Failing to address what all the students have already observed communicates that bullying behavior is inevitable. Even imperfect attempts at challenging bullying can communicate that the way in which we treat one another matters and that doing so in the classroom, hallways, playground, and buses is a priority worthy of our time and attention.

As I have already shared, teasing and harassment are issues that cannot be ignored or accepted as part of "growing up." We cannot wait for our schools to experience shootings, such as those at Columbine, to respond seriously to students becoming marginalized and excluded. Creating students who can pass tests but who treat one another cruelly is not a formula for successful schooling.

Teachers of young children rarely need convincing that the social climate of the classroom is crucial to students' development and learning. Teachers of older students often feel constrained by curriculums that squeeze out time for attending to the classroom's social climate. Fortunately, some high schools are realizing the importance of finding the balance between reaching state standards and testing goals and spending time helping students acquire pro-social skills.

Raising Awareness

"Look who it is," Rodney said, watching Darrell approach. "There's the punk who's been hiding from me," Tyray said. "Boy, you better have some money for me, 'cause I've lost all my patience with you." He walked over to Darrell and stared down into his face. "Watcha got, fool?"

This conversation from *The Bully* by Paul Langan (Townsend Press, 2001) is unfortunately not uncommon. It demonstrates the aggressive behavior a bully will use to intimidate his or her victims. Helping a bully change his or her behavior first requires raising awareness of that behavior and its effect on others. Raising awareness can lead to an understanding and then a greater sensitivity toward the consequences of their behavior toward others. Depending on the grade level, one effective way to begin this process is either by reading a book to the class or by having them read a book that addresses bullying, such as *The Bully*. (The Resources section on p. 174 lists other books that you can use in the classroom, which can help raise student awareness as well as educate them.)

Using graphic organizers to assist students' learning of the material they read is very helpful. Sample graphic organizers that can be used with these books appear on several Web sites, including http://www.ReadWriteThink.org. After filling out a graphic organizer, hold a class discussion about the ramifications of bullying behavior and ways to resolve conflicts.

Communicating with Compassion

Some students learn to bully because they have been subjected to mean and unfair behavior by others at home or elsewhere. This is unfortunate and sad but it's not an excuse to continue the aggressive patterns bullies choose to carry on. Everyone can choose to act in new and kinder ways. It is never too late to begin the awareness process with your students. Expectations should never be underestimated. Your viewpoint as a professional educator carries a tremendous amount of weight with your students. Be careful with the comments you make when talking to a bully. Statements such as "If you continue this behavior, you'll probably end up in jail" can be proven right by your student. Even though the bullies in your classroom may be some of the most unpleasant students to be around, they all have the potential to learn and change.

Communicating with compassion gives the message that it's their behavior that is unacceptable, not the bully as a person and your student. Separating the student from the behavior will require thought and self-discipline. It doesn't come easily. Old, unhelpful language, such as "What's wrong with you?" or "Why can't you just be nice to others?", is easy to throw at a student but wounds the spirit. Find language that educates and nourishes self-esteem. When talking to a bully, demonstrate the kind of respectful communication that you hope they will use with you and their peers. For example: "Jim, you are so mean to others!" vs. "Jim, calling Rowan carrothead is disrespectful talk and I won't allow it in this class."

To help reinforce positive behavior, you can use behavior contracts with students. Page 106 shows a sample of a behavior contract.

Identifying Bullies

The first step in ending bullying behavior in your school is to identify the bullies. Use the checklist on page 107 to help you find the students that most need your help to change their bullying ways.

KEEP UP!

_____

Student's Name

KEEP UP the behavior described below:

◇ _____

◇ _____

◇ _____

◇ _____

Date _____

_____   _____
Teacher's signature   Parent's signature

Identifying Bullies: Checklist

There are many warning signs that point to a student who may be bullying others in school or at home. The following checklist can help identify bullies or potential bullies in your school.

Student's name: _____ Date:_____

Teacher filling out checklist: _____

School Observations

_____ Seems bored with schoolwork

_____ Is usually physically larger than peers

_____ Very competitive with peers and dislikes losing

_____ Argues with adults and generally defiant toward authority

_____ Has a clique of peers who follow along with whatever he or she wants to do

_____ Lacks interest or concern for others

_____ Lacks interest in school-sponsored activities

_____ Gets excited when conflicts arise with other students

_____ Stays on the sideline while watching conflicts

_____ Enjoys manipulative power and control over peers

_____ Constantly testing limits with adults

Social-Emotional Behavior

_____ Blames others for aggressive behavior: "He asked for it"

_____ Exhibits a flat affect, little emotional expression

_____ Is frequently anxious and impulsive

_____ Exhibits little or no remorse for negative behavior

_____ Aggressive responses to direct questions from adults and peers

_____ Projects "coolness" and inner security

_____ Talks about hurting others

Finding Support

Communicating with other staff and adults is a key element in getting support for effective behavior interventions. Constant staff response to bullying behavior tells young people which behaviors are unacceptable.

Staff schoolwide should ask for support from students by encouraging them to report aggression rather than focusing on reducing "tattling." In one school I worked with there is a "code of silence" among students. This code creates an intrinsic norm, which gives the message, "If you tell anyone you're being harassed, it will get worse for you." Staff need to be trained to understand the importance of creating and expecting an open communication between them and their students without their students fearing retaliation by the bullies.

There are several ways in which staff training can take place. Once a month during staff meetings can be devoted to bully prevention and creating open communication with students and teachers. You can create a school bully prevention committee to oversee efforts to reduce aggression. The goals of any training should include:

- Educating staff

- Overseeing the effectiveness of the program

- Suggested changes

- Monitoring the consistency of interventions

Not unlike working with victims, most schools have a counselor whose responsibility is to meet with students who may be having behavior problems or who need support with external problems that are affecting their schoolwork such as parent conflicts, their pet just died, or they are having conflicts with friends and cannot concentrate on doing school- or homework. In my school district we call these helpers adjustment counselors.

Working with a student who is bullying others and exhibiting behavioral problems is significantly different than other problems students may have. Depending on the severity and extent of the bullying behavior, the school counselor can help the student understand cause-and-effect thinking and promote conscience development. The counselor can also be a support to teachers by providing specific instructions for working with the aggressive student around these issues. We help young people see connections between what they do and what happens to them through using predictable and transparent logical consequences. The counselor can do this through discussion, reflection and behavior management interventions.

The Flow Chart

The Flow Chart (p. 110) is an example of a logical consequence flow chart that can be used to increase awareness of cause-and-effect thinking and behavior.

Name _____   Date _____

The Flow Chart

Behavior _____

❏ Responsible   ❏ Not Responsible

Directions: On the line above write the behavior you are going to chart. Check either Responsible or Not Responsible to show what kind of behavior it is. Next, in each box below, write down the logical consequences to the behavior.

Example:

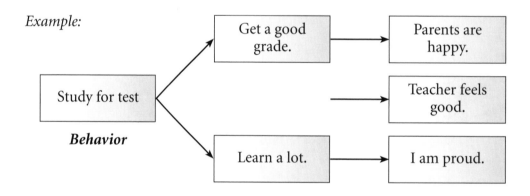

Your Flow Chart:

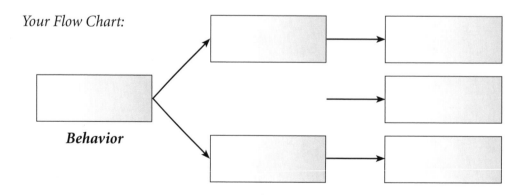

From *The Inclusive Classroom* by SiriNam Khalsa (Tucson, AZ: Good Year Books, 2005), p. 99.

For Teachers: Helping Families of Bullies

Bullying at Home

These facts support the importance of early intervention with students who exhibit bully behaviors. Bullies as well as their victims are at risk for a variety of social and behavior problems, including social isolation, failure in school, and emotional disturbance, such as depression. This makes it even more important that teachers and school staff keep the lines of communication open with parents.

It's important to remember that bullies often come from homes where there is little warmth and parental attention. They may be one-parent homes where the mother or father needs to work several odd-hour jobs to make ends meet. Effective loving parenting takes time and self-discipline, which many of these families lack. For example, parents who devote time to their children even when it is not demanded by misbehaviors will know when their child is in need of correction, reprimand, or praise, which they will administer with thoughtfulness and care. (Being a parent of two young children, I'm acutely aware of the fact that this is the goal that I strive to reach but do not always accomplish.) Healthy parenting takes time to make minor corrections and adjustments, listening to children, responding to them, giving them reminders and little lectures on right and wrong, little stories, hugs and kisses, and pats on the back. Parents model self-discipline, which requires reflection and control of one's thinking and behavior.

> ### Facts about Bullies
>
> ◇ *Studies suggest that aggressive behavior during childhood (from 6 to 13 years) may be a risk factor for future problems with violence and delinquency.*
>
> ◇ *Bullying is the entry-level behavior for physically aggressive acts.*
>
> ◇ *Some youths progress from bullying others to fighting with gangs to engaging in more violent behavior (e.g., assault, rape).*
>
> ◇ *Childhood bullies are at an increased risk for criminal convictions and involvement in serious recidivist crime as adults.*

Homes of children who are bullying may be homes where parents discipline inconsistently using physical punishment and erratic emotional outbursts as a means for control. They often exhibit little empathy or trust in others and have difficulty delaying their need for immediate gratification. This process is essential for children to learn as they grow into adolescents. For example, children learn to eat a meal before having dessert. By middle school, students should be able to complete their homework before watching television without parental prompting.

Students who exhibit behavior problems are also those who have not acquired the necessary discipline for delaying their need for immediate gratification. Despite average intelligence, their grades are poor, usually because they do little or no work. They skip classes in high school or skip school entirely on the whim of the moment. Their impulsiveness spills over into their social lives as well. They lack the control that is necessary to change aggressive behaviors toward their peers, and they grow up into adults who lack the social skills necessary for successful marriages and parenting. The reasons for this pathology is not fully known but most signs point to the quality of parenting they experienced as the possible determinant.

Parents of bullies often serve as undisciplined role models for their children. They are the "Do as I say, not as I do" parental model. They may have substance abuse problems and fight with each other in front of their children without restraint, dignity, or rationality. On more than one occasion, I have witnessed parents who have come into school to settle a dispute with a teacher, administrator, or a peer of their child and began exhibiting the same unacceptable behaviors that their child is in trouble for at school. They then proceeded to lecture their child about getting into trouble. Because parents are often godlike figures to children, children figure that the way their parents behave is the way they should behave toward others.

However, it is equally important to understand that there are also children who have bullied others that come from normal households with well-intentioned parents and relatively supportive environments. Understanding the basic family dynamics could help you with your approach and communication with parents you'll be helping.

Helping parents of bullies can be a challenging proposition but an essential one. Regardless of the cards they where dealt in life, it is essential to communicate with these parents with the same respect and dignity that you would with any parent. I feel that it is important to say this because I've noticed an unfortunate tendency for some teachers and administrators to talk down to parents that are having difficulty raising their children and/or controlling themselves.

Communicating with Parents

1. Informing Parents: It is not unusual for parents to be defensive when a teacher or administrator wants to talk. Some parents deny there is a problem and others get angry that their child has been branded as the "troublemaker." Some parents withdraw and feel very sad and guilty. You can be a calming influence and help reduce their fears, build trust, and encourage their ability to cooperate by demonstrating your desire to be partners in dealing with the problem at hand. Following is a sample conversation between a teacher and a parent, discussing the parent's child.

Teacher: Hello, Mrs. Simon. This is Mr. Levine, Jim's teacher. I'm calling because Jim has been caught harassing another student in school and I wanted your help in dealing with this before it gets out of hand.

Parent: I work odd hours and just got a new job. I haven't had the time I'd like to have to spend with Jim. This is surprising. Are you sure Jim is bothering other kids? Jim usually tells me things are going well in school.

Teacher: I understand. Yes, I'm sure this is happening because he was seen by a teacher, Ms. Jackson, knocking books out of another student's arms. That student has been complaining about this. Can we set up a meeting for you to come to school so we can decide on the best way to proceed?

Parent: OK. How about this Thursday?

Teacher: Fine. I'll see you at 3:00.

Parent: Should Jim be there?

Teacher: Why don't we adults talk first and then bring him in on the next meeting?

Parent: OK.

Teacher: Great. I look forward to talking with you and thank you for your cooperation.

2. The Meeting: It's important when discussing a student's problem behaviors with a parent that you always mention some positive attributes the child has exhibited as well. Once you've described the behaviors, you can move the conversation into possible issues at home, in the neighborhood, and at school that may be creating these problems. For example, living with one parent who works odd hours can be stressful for any child. It's not unusual for these children to be asked to watch younger siblings when the parent is working. This could cause resentment and pent-up anger that the student may release on another innocent student at school.

> **Key Concept**
>
> *It's always best to give students some control on your terms than have them take it on theirs.*

As the student's teacher, you may provide new observations and insight that will help the parents better understand and resolve the situation. Ideally, you, the parent, and the student will all contribute ideas on how to solve the problem of bullying younger and smaller students as quickly as possible. Be open-minded as you share and discuss strategies; then decide by consensus which to implement. If the student is part of the problem solving, he or she is much more apt to agree to work on the solutions versus being told that he or she has no choice.

The first step to stopping Jim's bullying is helping him accept responsibility for his behavior. It is not unusual for a student bully to avoid the pain of his or her problems by saying, "This is not my problem. It's caused by other people so they have the problem." Having parents talk to the student with the teacher present can be very helpful when the student is in denial of his or her behaviors.

Here's another sample conversation between teacher and parent:

Teacher: Hi, Mrs. Simon. Thank you for coming. I've asked Ms. Jackson to join us. As I mentioned, she observed Jim bullying another student in the hallway.

Ms. Jackson: Jim walked up to another boy who is smaller than he is and in sixth grade and purposefully knock his books out of the boy's arms and then laughed with two other boys who were walking with him. When I asked Jim to help pick up the books, he gave me a dirty look and said it was just an accident. The other boy was very upset and said it happens a lot.

Parent: Does this happen all the time?

Teacher: No, it doesn't. There are times when I see Jim acting responsibly in class and having a friendly conversation with his peers. But as I mentioned, this younger and smaller student has been complaining to his sixth-grade teacher about being bothered by Jim. When I asked Jim if there was a problem between him and the other student, he acted as if nothing was occurring.

Parent: Well, what do you think is going on?

Teacher: I think Jim is exhibiting bullying behaviors that go beyond playful teasing. They are hurtful and creating fear in this student's day. I also think that Jim can change, but it will take all of us to support this change.

3. **Possible Solutions:** Once the student accepts responsibility, then generating possible solutions can take place. For example:

◇ Jim may volunteer to work with the other student in a subject that is difficult for that student or have lunch with the student on certain days of the week (This requires adult supervision and willingness on both students' parts.)

◇ Jim may agree to actively avoid the other student whenever possible.

◇ He can also agree to participate in classes with the school adjustment counselor or teacher and complete the activities in this book.

◇ If the bullying continues, discuss logical consequences, such as Billy needing to be escorted to and from classes by a teacher, paraprofessional, or administrator.

◇ He can be limited to certain areas of the school until a change of attitude and behavior is exhibited.

You should have ongoing communication with the parents. Once you have all agreed on the interventions or action plan and to work together as a team, agree on times during the next several weeks that you can discuss, by phone, the progress of the plan and the possible need to meet again. E-mail may be the most efficient way to communicate, if both of you have access. As the student demonstrates positive change, you can move weekly communication to twice a month and so on until the problem behaviors have stopped.

If the student accepts responsibility at school, you can have the student communicate to his or her parents by explaining the problem and agreed-upon solution in a letter. Read the letter for accuracy before it goes home. A response from the student's parents in the form of a signed note or phone call is also necessary.

How to Interview a Bully

Part of the process of helping the family of a bully is interviewing the student. Starting the interview process and putting light on the problem often will change behaviors.

During the interview, you must clearly state in a nonjudgmental way that the school will not tolerate bullying and other aggressive behaviors. It may be helpful to discuss and acknowledge the results of bullying behavior on themselves and others. Exploring the reasons why Mark is bullying others is a beginning to finding ways to change his aggressive behaviors. Some questions that you can ask include:

- Does anyone that you know pick on you?

- How do other kids bother you?

- Is it hard for you to control your temper?

- How does it feel to be able to have power over younger or smaller kids?

- Do you have many friends? What do friends do and not do?

Do: Acknowledge that you can't make him or her do something, but instead ask for his or her help. Offer limited choices. Be firm but empathetic. Set a time for practicing the new behaviors and follow-through with the action plan—for example, helping the student learn ways to control his or her temper or tell the student who to go to when he or she can't.

Don't: Intensify the behavior by arguing with the student, retaliate by punitive reactions, or give up on the bully.

The meeting should result in an action plan (see p. 121) that provides a clear and consistent set of behavioral expectations that need to be enforced. If the student would prefer to work with another teacher he or she respects or trusts, someone he or she can talk to, let the student know that you can set up a meeting with that adult.

The following scenario is a sample interview that can act as a guide for your discussion with someone who you suspect might be bullying other students.

Adult: Mark, can we sit and talk about something that I've been wanting to discuss with you?

Student: Yeah, I guess so.

Adult: Good. Let's meet next period.

Adult (later): I've noticed you're having some difficulty being around some students during lunch.

Student: Who are you talking about? That little squirt?

Adult: Well, if you're referring to Jonathan, yes.

Student: He's so nerdy.

Adult: So, he really irritates you to the point where you bother him?

Student: Yeah. I can't stand the way he looks at me and the way he talks.

Adult: I understand. But Mark, the way you are choosing to deal with your feelings about him is not acceptable. Picking on other kids will not be tolerated in our school.

Student: Well, maybe he should move.

Adult: Mark, that's not your decision. Would you like to learn ways to avoid Jonathan—or not to let him get you so upset? Because the other choice is that you will get into real trouble.

Student: How can you help?

Adult: We can start with agreeing on the problem that needs to be worked on and then write up an "Action Plan" or plan how we can work together to change your behavior. Do you want my help?

Student: I guess so.

Adult: Okay. I think you made a good choice. I'll let your parents know that we are working on this problem and I'll get back to you today on when we will meet again.

For Parents: Helping Your Child Who May Be a Bully

Here are several tools and strategies for parents whose child is exhibiting bullying behavior at school:

◇ Listen to your children. Encourage them to talk about school, other peers in their school, and things that may be bothering them. If you let the child lead the conversation, where it ends up is often very different than where it ends up. For instance, it may go from being annoyed at another student, to resentments about a teacher, to your child's desire to make new friends. Detect things that your child might say that may indicate bullying behavior (e.g., "I don't like wimpy kids who complain all the time").

◇ Don't bully your child physically or verbally. Talk to your child in a firm voice without yelling at him or her when he or she misbehaves.

◇ Help your child find ways to manage his or her anger (e.g., sports, drawing, using clay, talking, walking, hitting a pillow). Make it perfectly clear that bullying behavior will not be tolerated.

◇ Spend extra time with your child. Schedule activities that you both enjoy doing together and monitor his or her activities at home, in the neighborhood, and at school.

◇ Teach your child alternative ways to solve problems. Teach him or her to handle situations without violent words or actions (see "One-on-One Problem-solving Meeting," below).

◇ Provide nonviolent outlets for your child's entertainment. Avoid violent video games, TV programs, and toys that promote aggressive behavior. Involve your child in different kinds of special activities, such as martial arts, music, and sports, that will help them gain self-confidence and respect for other children.

◇ At bedtime, talk to your child about his or her day. In addition, organize your child's mornings so that the day begins on a positive note rather than in a hurried, erratic manner that invites arguments.

Empowering Interventions

One-on-One Problem-solving Meeting

When your student is caught bullying, providing consequences for their misbehavior may have only temporary results. Your student may need to receive more in-depth guidance from you or another adult. Having a one-on-one problem-solving meeting is an opportunity to listen to the student's concerns, firmly clarify your expectations, and work together on an action plan.

I like the guidelines for conducting a problem-solving meeting that Lee Canter (Lee Canter & Associates) suggests. The following steps will help you conduct a thorough meeting that educates the student with respect while directly addressing the bullying problem.

1. **Meet with the student in a private place.** A student who is dealing with behavioral problems wants to feel that what is talked about is confidential and not reported to the "whole school." The meeting should be relatively short, no longer than 30 minutes.

2. **Demonstrate empathy and concern.** Instead of getting angry at the student, focus on helping them learn and understand why he or she needs to choose alternative behaviors. Effective problem solving starts with the adult who can empathize with their student and allow the logical consequences of the student's behaviors to sink in. This approach demonstrates your concern and caring for the student's well-being. The student needs to believe that you do not want to punish or embarrass them.

3. **Question the student.** Remember, the first step toward changing behavior is accepting responsibility for the behavior. Ask the student questions that will give you the opportunity to listen and determine how close he or she is to understanding that there is a problem and that he or she must take responsibility for causing it. Questions can include: "Do you think everything is going well for you in school? Why do you think you're having difficulty with some of the students in the school? What part of the problem do you think you can change?"

4. **Determine how the student, with your help, can improve his or her behavior.** Be careful not to become a rescuer. Focus the meeting on what the student can choose to do differently in the future that will help him or her to change their negative behavior pattern. Talk about the bullying situation and, if needed, teach some alternative behaviors and ways of thinking.

5. **State clearly your expectations.** Empathetic and caring communication also includes communicating the seriousness of the bullying behavior and that it must not continue. The student must understand that under no circumstances will you or any other teacher allow bullying behavior to be part of the school community.

6. **Decide on an Action Plan.** An action plan (see the Action Plan Form on p. 121) consists of one or two observable behaviors that need changing and a time line in which the change will take place. Include any supports, such as daily meetings with you or scheduled meetings with the school counselor. Give copies of the action plan to the student and his or her parents. Schedule a follow-up meeting to determine if any progress has been made.

Used with permission. From *Assertive Discipline: Positive Behavior Management for Today's Classroom*, 3rd Edition by Lee Canter and Marlene Canter, pp. 193–197. Copyright 2001, 1992, 1976 by Solution Tree (formerly National Educational Service), 304 West Kirkwood Avenue, Bloomington, Indiana 47404, 800-733-6786, www.solution-tree.com.

Action Plan Form

Student's name: _____ Age: _____ Grade: _____

Name of teacher filling out form: _____

Today's date: _____

Describe problem: _____

_____

_____

Define goal: _____

_____

_____

Action Plan:

1. Observable Behavior	Supports	Dates

2. Observable Behavior	Supports	Dates

Follow-up meeting date: _____

Releasing Anger

Ask your student(s) if they were ever told to count to 10 when they were angry. Explain that this strategy can be used to cool down when upset. The reason it can work is that your mind tells your body what to do and your breath helps your mind relax.

Draw this diagram on the chalkboard:

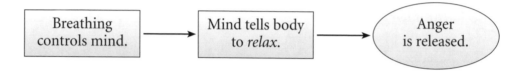

Breathing controls mind. → Mind tells body to *relax*. → Anger is released.

Now it's time for the student(s) to practice this releasing anger strategy. Encourage them to try this counting and breathing technique the next time they become angry and feel like bothering one of their peers.

When practicing this breathing, you can say the following:

"When someone gets you angry or your mind is telling to you harass someone, try doing the following exercise. Take a long, deep inhalation and at the same time say the number 1 to yourself. Then let go of any anger by relaxing your body when you exhale. Now inhale and say 2, exhaling and relaxing. You're doing really well. Concentrate and repeat this process until you get to 10. I'll watch and see who is following the directions."

Ask them to experiment with this and report back to you on how it worked. Remind them that practice makes perfect.

Start a Bully Patrol

Positive peer pressure can be a powerful tool in helping bullies change their behavior. One way is to form a group of students whose objective in the school is to look out for bullying behavior in school. When they see someone being harrassed in any way (when a teacher is not around or focusing on something else in the classroom or in the hallway), the bully patrol shouts out in unison, "Stop bothering (student's name)!" The administration must be supportive of this intervention as well. It's also helpful to role-play how this would work in the classroom and in the school community.

Practicing what they may say to another person who is bullying someone will help students to respond quickly in an assertive manner. For example: "We don't tease each other at John F. Kennedy Middle School," "When you bother Sam, you're also bothering me, and I don't like that," "Can you stop being so mean to her?", "Bullying is not cool, so stop bothering Carly."

Supporting peers helping peers makes a lot of sense but will take planning and collaboration with other adults. Students want to learn how to administer justice to someone who has "broken the respect laws" of their school. Some schools set up weekly courts where a teacher acts as a chairperson and classmates as the jury. The teacher ensures that the court rules are followed and "sentences" are fair and equitable.

Building Self-esteem

A lot has been written about the benefits and questions concerning supporting self-esteem with our children. I want to first separate myth from fact when addressing this important topic. In their book *Stick Up for Yourself!: Every Kid's Guide to Personal Power and Positive Self-esteem* (Free Spirit Publishing, 2001), Kaufman, Raphael, and Espeland clearly explain that self-esteem isn't about feeling superior to other people. It's about you and how you feel about yourself. When someone has high self-esteem, they are more likely to resist negative peer pressure and do what is right for all involved. Feeling strong enables them to cope with the challenges and pressures in life.

Self-esteem Myths and Facts

MYTH	FACT
Self-esteem comes from outside of you—from people always complimenting and praising you.	Self-esteem comes from inside—from knowing yourself and the kind of person you want to be.
Self-esteem makes you weak and unable to deal with life's challenges.	Without self-esteem you will always have difficulty with effectively meeting and dealing with life's difficulties.
Self-esteem can be given and taken away.	Self-esteem is learned and earned.

Common Signs of Low Self-esteem

- Whining
- Cheating in games
- Teasing
- Complaining
- Overpleasing
- Criticism avoidant
- Blaming
- Withdrawn

- Exaggerated bragging
- Exhibiting physical and verbal aggression
- Always clowning and acting overly silly
- Lack of empathy toward others
- Unable to make choices or solve problems
- Expressing a narrow range of emotions
- Demeaning one's own talents
- Exhibiting anti-social behaviors

Self-esteem-building Activities. There are many activities that will help students feel better about themselves. Here are some examples that you can implement with your students:

1. **Student of the Week:** This simple activity can have powerful results and has been around for many years. I've used it and seen teachers use it in the elementary and middle-school grades with success. Adapting this activity for high school-aged students is not only possible but highly recommended.

   Place all students' names on slips of paper in a box. Each week, ask a student to pick a name out of the box. Write the chosen student's name on top of a large piece of newsprint taped to the wall. Start by expressing a few positive qualities about the student, such as:

   - Rashard enjoys reading.
   - Caitlin wears really nice clothes.
   - Antonio is kind to everyone.
   - Ravi shares his things.
   - Angela is a great dancer.

   Then ask your students to take turns writing a list of positive qualities about the chosen student. Write the list under the Student of the Week's name. Some teachers take a photo of the student and tape it on top of the list. You can do this activity monthly as well.

I always ask students to take turns stating what they like about the Student of the Week by looking at him or her and stating it directly. For example, someone might say, "Peter, I really like the way you play sports," and then Peter would acknowledge the compliment by saying "Thank you."

Remind students that it could be their turn in the future and they should express something positive about their classmate.

2. **Daily Success List:** Ask students to write down three things in their "Daily Success Book" that they learned or did today that made them feel good about themselves. Examples include:

- I helped John clean up in Art class.

- I got a good grade on my test.

- I met a new friend today.

- I ask a question without shouting out.

- I came to school on time.

- I tried out for the basketball team.

- I took my first guitar lesson.

3. **A Random Act of Kindness:** Explain to your class that random means unplanned and that being kind builds character, or who we are. Being kind also creates a safe and pleasant school environment. Before class begins, ask students to state an example of a "random act of kindness." Before the end of the day ask students to state an example of a "random act of kindness" that they *participated in, experienced*, or *observed* during the day.

4. **Helping Others in Need:** On his way to giving one of many keynote speeches to a group of teachers in training, 2003 Massachusetts Teacher of the Year Jeff Ryan was thinking about what would be one of the most important things he could share with these future teachers. To summarize what he shared: "Reading and writing are very important. The sciences and history of this world are equally valuable, but a lesson that is priceless is teaching our students and future citizens that they are not the center of the universe. Our children must understand that the world doesn't revolve around their needs but that there are many others in need of much more."

Many schools collect clothing and cans of food for the local survival centers during the holidays but one teacher I worked with always had a "Helping Others in Need" box in her classroom. She asked students to bring in canned food and clothing that would be donated when the box was full (which happened very often). All the students were asked to write thank-you letters to the center for "giving me the opportunity to help others in need." This wise teacher understood the character benefits her students would receive by experiencing the act of helping others.

Getting Students Beyond Separateness. It is my belief that the inherent paradox with low self-esteem (and the bully personality) is that the person is focusing too much on their own needs and self. "Why me?", "How come I don't have friends?", "I never get to have fun like them," "I can't do that," "She won't get away with that," "I can't stand that nerd," or "She's stuck up." People who have a low sense of self also feel separate from others. Students need a teacher who will manage opportunities that will give them a different experience of life.

What follows in the quality of their helping others in need when they begin to know themselves beyond separateness? Perhaps, at the very least, they can be a little less fearful, and a little more trusting. When your students have an experience of giving—which is a taste of unity with others who they may not normally associate with—they're that much more ready to bring it into any situation, at any given moment, with anybody.

Helping Students See Their Behaviors. Bullies are involved in their emotional reactions toward others and have difficulty reflecting on their behaviors. Thinking before they act is essential, but this skill needs to be practiced. The first step is having some understanding of how their mind works. Most students don't realize that they can control their *feelings* by controlling their *thoughts*. For example, if they are feeling sad it may be because they are thinking of their dog who recently got hit by a car or when their father left the house and didn't return. If they think of other things like a birthday party or the new bike they just got, their feelings will change. Through the awareness of the cognitive or thinking part of their mind, they can then work on modifying their behavior.

Try this with students:

Imagine that your mind is like the sky, and that across it pass thoughts as clouds. The sky is always present: It contains the clouds and yet is not contained by them.

With practice, this image of the separation of mind and thoughts can help your students change a negative thought whenever they choose to. Bullies are never impartial. They have a mental habit of being attached, prejudiced, and closed-minded. The thought "I can't stand that kid" changed to "Well I don't need to bother with him and get into more trouble" can also change anger into impartiality.

Teaching Imagery. Michael Jordan once said, "I use the power of my mind to overcome my limitations." Help your students become masters of their minds versus slaves of their negative thoughts. Teach them to see or imagine themselves getting along with other kids they are having difficulty with and might want to harass.

Imagery, or seeing pictures in the mind, is crucial to education. Imagine trying to read without picturing things; doing a geometry problem without seeing the symbols in your head. One English teacher relaxed her students and then guided them on a mountain hike. Suddenly they saw a cave leading into the side of the mountain. She left them at the mouth of the cave with instructions to go inside and have an adventure. When they came back she instructed them to write their experiences in two pages. Reluctant writers were more than happy to get their thoughts on paper. In the same way you can use visualization to help your students change their unwanted behaviors. With daily practice they can change negative thought patterns by replacing them with accepting thoughts that can become behaviors. Remember, your student(s) need to be ready and willing to practice this if it is going to work for them. Here are some sample visualization exercises:

⬧ **Knowing Your Mind:** "Sit comfortably with your back straight but not rigid. Simply let your thoughts move in and out of your mid. I want you to try and look at your thoughts without staying with them too long and getting involved with them. It's kind of like watching TV. If you are feeling a little tense trying to watch your mind, relax. The sky doesn't get all tense trying to see the clouds. See your thoughts passing by and just notice them and say goodbye. Be the blue sky behind your thoughts."

⬧ **Positive Self:** "Today we are going to practice seeing ourselves being successful in school. Sit comfortably with your back straight but not rigid. Imagine yourself sitting in the lunchroom and a classmate who really annoys you is looking at you. You feel yourself getting upset and your thoughts are telling you to go over to that student and confront him or her. (Pause) Now see yourself controlling your negative thoughts by telling yourself that the other student may just be looking your way for no real reason. You tell yourself that 'I'm just going to ignore him or her and enjoy my lunch.' See yourself eating and enjoying your lunch with other classmates while your feelings about the other student change to feeling annoyed to not caring. Now see yourself walking past that student in the hallway and thinking, 'I'm just going to walk by him or her and not cause any trouble.' Imagine yourself walking by that student feeling good about your positive behavior and the control you have over your negative thinking."

◇ **What's Next?:** "For today's writing assignment I want you to first sit comfortably with your back straight but not too rigid. Imagine yourself outside on the playing field and a student who tends to annoy you is walking with someone you like. They are walking toward you and you have to decide how you're going to interact with both classmates without creating a problem or hurting someone's feelings. Both students approach you. . . . (Pause) Now write down what comes next and use as much of the page as you want to finish your story."

Students can share their stories with a partner and volunteers can be asked to read them to the whole class. Give feedback to every student about their imagined response to this situation. If the bully student has a negative ending to his or her story, you may want to make a brief comment, such as, "That's unfortunate that you would choose to react that way. Let's talk about it later." Then privately use the negative response as a means to discuss the bullying problem. Conversely, if the class bully writes a positive imagery response, acknowledge him or her in front of peers for the mature decision he or she would have made.

Keeping Our Schools Safe

"An ounce of prevention is worth a pound of cure."

Anger in the Halls

As mentioned earlier, many of the aggressive incidents toward innocent victims occur when teachers are not in the immediate vicinity. An alarming number of students express discomforting aggressive feelings through their body language and behavior in school hallways. It was not long ago that these expressions of anger might well have gone unnoticed, but the string of deadly shootings that have occurred in the recent past at schools across the country are radically altering how we interact with our students. We can agree that the time has arrived for a proactive approach toward violence prevention, rather than an ineffective reactive plan. We cannot continue to address the issue of aggression in our halls and the challenges our students confront in the same way as we used to.

Are Security Precautions Sufficient?

Surveillance equipment and metal detectors are becoming a normal part of every school environment but their effectiveness is questionable. Metal detectors did not stop an incident of violence at the Capitol Building in Washington, DC. A security guard who lost his life to a lone gunman who walked right through the detectors. Even though these systems may be somewhat of a deterrent, we know that if a middle school- or high school-aged student wants to bring a weapon to school, he or she can use a buddy to sneak the weapon through the metal detector by clandestinely passing it on the ground. Students who do witness this often choose not to say anything out of fear of retaliation.

We may not be able to stop every act of violence in our schools; however, we can and must reduce the number of violent acts by incorporating guidelines and steps emphasizing an assertive response identifying early warning signs and effective interventions.

Alternative Solutions

Many schools are deciding to take a different approach toward dealing with their troubled youth. These schools are offering increased access to school counselors; others have hired staff specifically for peer mediation and violence prevention. Students who are identified as exhibiting potentially violent behavior are being directed into anger management classes and outside supportive therapy. In many of today's urban middle and high schools, it is not unusual to see a police officer walking the halls who is especially trained in communicating with adolescents.

Reactions to the various interventions have been varied. Many teachers and parents embrace the idea of increased physical security and believe that the very concept of security may also reduce a student's personal freedom. Other parents and teachers are concerned about the culture of an excessively secure school environment. They don't like the idea of their children having little choice but to be searched by school officials. They can appreciate the schools' positive intentions but think schools are missing the mark. These people don't want to turn their schools into prison-like environments where students are searched and watched all day by adults and cameras. These parents and teachers want safe schools as well but without losing a nurturing learning community that encourages communication and creativity.

We can all agree that security precautions are needed for safe and secure schools. However, experience tells us that it's prudent to also put our efforts into identifying and intervening before violence occurs and students needlessly become victims. Experts say fostering strong relationships and open communication between students and adults can be a more effective deterrent to school violence than installing metal detectors and guards at the front doors.

Trusting relationships between staff and students is what helped Principal William Gummerson when he thwarted a possible shooting in Northwestern High School in Rock Hill, S.C. There were no overt warning signs that could have triggered an intervention procedure to prevent a potential act of violence. Fortunately, fellow classmates reported that a boy had shown them a gun before school. The principal found the handgun and bullets in a box near the boy's desk.

> **Key Concept**
>
> *If students trust the adults at school, they're more likely to confide in them when trouble is brewing.*

This kind of student is difficult to detect and will almost always be a surprise to everyone involved. He was angry at his peers and school community for not intervening in problems he was experiencing with others. It was the student-teacher communication that proved to be the most effective intervention. Security personnel who are trained to work with children and understand peer pressure and networking can also help schools keep informed about potentially violent problems.

Prevention: A Proactive Approach

The key to preventing violence in our schools is to become vigilant in identifying students who may be at risk at some for violent behavior. When school personnel have identified warning signs, they can determine a level of intervention to meet the student's needs. The prevention model includes:

◇ **Four levels of intervention,** which correlate with each group of warning signs and act as guidelines for your school to follow in response to a student's behavior. Levels 1–3 can be followed through to completion, if necessary, or ended at any point, considering the student's progress.

◇ **Self-help building exercises** are additional activities for all students who need support in finding alternative ways of controlling anger and resolving conflicts as well as developing self-esteem and responsible social skills.

Warning Signs and Interventions

The behavior or language listed as warning signs for each level threat below, such as threatening to harm someone, is identified as a *spark event*. The spark event is the trigger to verbal threats and could help identify the underlying causes. Looking objectively at the cause(s) is the key to supporting the change necessary for ending the intervention.

Using an Intervention Form can support your objectivity when reporting and analyzing the best follow-up intervention. In the case of verbal threats, a designated staff member would fill out the Level 1 Intervention Form (pp. 134–136) for the purpose of identifying initial warning signs, possible causes, a follow-up action plan, and an evaluation of interventions. For example, a colleague once found a letter in the classroom written by one of his students. The letter had some very violent language directed toward the teacher. He became very upset and consequently lost his objectivity, which understandably created additional problems. An Intervention Form would have been a practical tool that helped support the professionalism necessary when emotions where running high. Each level has a designated intervention form, which is filled out by a designated staff member.

Normally, we do not so much look at things as we overlook them. When a student is making verbal comments that have an aggressive tone to them, it is always best to intervene and find out why he or she is talking in this manner. Following are lists of warning signs and interventions designed to meet each group of signs:

Level 1: Threat of Harm to Others or Self

  Warnings:

    Verbal Threats (What Is Said)

- Life is not worth living.

- I'm going to kill myself.

- They won't get away with it.

- Just wait until after school.

- I'll show him or her what's up.

- I know where his car is.

- I'm going to blow him away.

Nonverbal

- Violent drawings that depict harmful acts

- Letters written with aggressive content

- E-mails suggesting violent acts

- Web sites that suggest violence

- Excessive feelings of rejection

- Social withdrawal

- Feelings of being picked on or harassed

- Clothing that is unusually dark and introverted

Body Language

- Clenched fists

- Direct stare

- Hands on hips

- Tense body

- Finger pointing

- Getting "in your face"

- Pacing and making aggressive comments

Intervention:

Level 1 Intervention addresses language that is aggressive in nature and suggestive of harm to oneself or others. Often a student who is expressing these types of comments needs a structured intervention that may include counseling, mediation, and/or anger management classes (e.g., self-help activities).

Level 1 Intervention Form

Verbal Threat of Harm to Others or Self

(CONFIDENTIAL)

School: _____

Student's name: _____

Grade: _____ D.O.B.: _____/_____/_____

ID Number: _____

Dominant language: _____

Date: _____

1. Who Initiated Intervention?

_____ Student

_____ Other Student: _____

_____ Teacher: _____

_____ Other: _____

2. Description of actual threatening language, including the *spark event*:

_____

_____

_____

_____

Initial Evaluation

I. Name: _____

Title: _____

Date of interview: _____ Report Attached: ____Yes ____No

II. Determined Concern of Risk:

_____ No Concern

_____ Minimal Concern

_____ Moderate Concern

_____ Major Concern

III. Explanation of Concern:

_____

_____

_____

_____

IV. People and/or Agency Notified:

Name(s): _____ Date: _____

Parental Meeting Scheduled for: Date: _____ Time: _____

Place: _____

V. Results of Meeting:

_____

_____

_____

Action Plan

I. Actions Taken:

_____ School decided no further action was necessary.

_____ Parents decided no further action was necessary.

_____ Student will be monitored over the next __ Week __ Month __ Other

_____ Student will receive support by:

_____ (a) Meeting with Counselor

_____ (b) Participate in Skills Classes

_____ (c) Referral made to Agency: _____

_____ (d) Peer Mediation

_____ (e) Other: _____

II. Evaluation of Progress: Date of Observation: _____ / _____ / _____

_____ Noticeable attitude change

_____ Noticeable mood change

_____ Appearance

_____ Social interactions with peers

_____ Interactions with teachers

_____ Change in academic performance

_____ Other _____

Additional Evaluation of Progress:

_____

_____

_____

_____

III. Intervention Termination by: _____

Date of Termination: _____ / _____ / _____

Level 2: Acts of Physical Violence with the Purpose of Causing Harm to Self or Others

Warnings:

- Hitting or punching others or self

- Kicking

- Biting

- Spitting

- Throwing objects

- Pulling of hair or clothing

- Pushing with aggressive intent

- Self-mutilation (with sharp object)

Interventions:

Level 2 Intervention addresses physically aggressive acts by a student toward another student or adult in the school. Level 2 goes beyond the verbalization or intent to cause harm. It is an observable escalation into behaviors that carry with them a greater risk to everyone involved.

The spark event of a physical attack will be varied. Violent acts usually begin with minor conflicts or disagreements that can lead to intense negative reactions. When a student becomes frustrated and loses the ability to think rationally, his or her reaction can turn into a spontaneous as well as a predetermined act of retaliation. In either case a potentially serious threat of harm exists and immediate intervention is necessary.

When implementing a Level 2 Intervention, it is sensible to isolate the student from the school population in order to minimize the chance of additional aggressive acts. Determining the level of control the student is showing will indicate the necessary level of immediate intervention. If a student *cannot* regain control of his or her behavior after a physical assault, then implement a more restrictive intervention and contact law enforcement.

Level 2 Intervention Form

Acts of Physical Violence

(CONFIDENTIAL)

School: _____

Student's name: _____

Grade: _____ D.O.B.: _____/_____/_____

ID Number: _____

Dominant language: _____

Date: _____

1. Who Initiated Intervention?

_____ Student

_____ Other Student: _____

_____ Teacher: _____

_____ Other: _____

2. Description of actual physical violence, including the *spark event*:

_____

_____

_____

_____

Initial Evaluation

I. Name: _____

Title: _____

Date of interview: _____ Report Attached: ___Yes ___No

II. Determined Concern of Risk:

_____ No Concern

_____ Minimal Concern

_____ Moderate Concern

_____ Major Concern

III. Explanation of Concern:

_____

_____

_____

_____

IV. People and/or Agency Notified:

Name(s): _____ Date: _____

Parental Meeting Scheduled for: Date: _____ Time: _____

Place: _____

V. Results of Meeting:

_____

_____

_____

_____

Action Plan

I. Actions Taken:

_____ School decided no further action was necessary.

_____ Parents decided no further action was necessary.

_____ Student will be monitored over the next __ Week __ Month __ Other

_____ Student will receive support by:

     _____ (a) Meeting with Counselor

     _____ (b) Participate in Skills Classes

     _____ (c) Referral made to Agency: _____

     _____ (d) Peer Mediation

     _____ (e) Other: _____

II. Evaluation of Progress: Date of Observation: _____/_____/_____

_____ Noticeable attitude change

_____ Noticeable mood change

_____ Appearance

_____ Social interactions with peers

_____ Interactions with teachers

_____ Change in academic performance

_____ Other _____

Additional Evaluation of Progress:

_____

_____

_____

_____

III. Intervention Termination by: _____

Date of Termination: _____/_____/_____

Level 3: Bringing a Weapon into School (without the Intent of Using It)

Warnings:

- Handgun

- Rifle

- Pocket knife

- Boot knife

- Kitchen knife

- Homemade weapons

- Sharp objects

- Razor blades

- Chains

- Homemade explosive device

Intervention:

Level 3 Intervention deals with a student bringing in a weapon without intending to use it. The research on violence is especially frightening when it comes to the number of weapons brought to school. An estimated 100,000 children and adolescents carry a weapon to school every day! In many cases it is the potential fear of being harassed or bullied that causes a student to bring a weapon for "protection" into school without the intent of using it. The potential for an accident to occur escalates significantly.

In many cases, a staff member learns of a weapon that has been brought to school by a student who overheard another student claim to have a weapon or showed it to a peer. At this point, most schools are obligated to notify the police department of potential harm. Isolate the student in question from the general student population and monitor him or her until the police arrive.

Level 3 Intervention Form

Bringing a Weapon into School (without Intent of Use)

(CONFIDENTIAL)

School: _____

Student's name: _____

Grade: _____ D.O.B.: _____/_____/_____

ID Number: _____

Dominant language: _____

Date: _____

1. Who Initiated Intervention?

_____ Student

_____ Other Student: _____

_____ Teacher: _____

_____ Other: _____

2. Description of weapon and circumstances surrounding its identification:

_____

_____

_____

_____

Initial Evaluation

I. Name: _____

Title: _____

Date of interview: _____ Report Attached: ___Yes ___No

II. Determined Concern of Risk:

_____ No Concern

_____ Minimal Concern

_____ Moderate Concern

_____ Major Concern

III. Explanation of Concern:

_____

_____

_____

_____

IV. People and/or Agency Notified:

Name(s): _____ Date: _____

Parental Meeting Scheduled for: Date: _____ Time: _____

Place: _____

V. Results of Meeting:

_____

_____

_____

_____

Action Plan

I. Actions Taken:

_____ School decided no further action was necessary.

_____ Parents decided no further action was necessary.

_____ Student will be monitored over the next __ Week __ Month __ Other

_____ Student will receive support by:

    _____ (a) Meeting with Counselor

    _____ (b) Participate in Skills Classes

    _____ (c) Referral made to Agency: _____

    _____ (d) Peer Mediation

    _____ (e) Other: _____

II. Evaluation of Progress: Date of Observation: ____/____/____

_____ Noticeable attitude change

_____ Noticeable mood change

_____ Appearance

_____ Social interactions with peers

_____ Interactions with teachers

_____ Change in academic performance

_____ Other _____

Additional Evaluation of Progress:

_____

_____

_____

_____

III. Intervention Termination by: _____

Date of Termination: ____/____/____

Level 4: Bringing a Weapon into School (with the Intent of Using It)

Warning and Actions:

- All weapons

- Call 911

- Implement crisis plan

Intervention:

The Level 4 Intervention is the school's crisis plan, which must be followed in a situation involving students who intend to use weapons they bring to school. If this situation occurs, the school must immediately respond by implementing a crisis plan.

Steps to Follow When a Crisis Occurs:

1. **Recognize and Assess** life and safety issues.

2. **Call 911** and notify police first followed by the fire department.

3. **Convene the Crisis Team** implementing the crisis plan (either Plan A or Plan B, on page 146).

4. **Maintain Awareness** of the students' locations and adult supervision assigned to each location.

5. **Coordinate and Disseminate Information** pertaining to the location of aggressor(s).

6. **Notify Parents** and any other appropriate people or agencies.

7. **Stay Focused** on meeting the security and safety needs of the entire school community.

The crisis plan is a guide to action used in the face of a serious threat. The plan follows a specific step-by-step format. Not unlike a fire drill, all school districts are wise to have a crisis plan developed with staff, police, and fire departments' input. Your school's crisis plan should be reviewed and practiced by the school community. Make parents aware of the plan as well. At the high school level, students could be included in being part of a designated team of staff and students with the objective of assessing the situation at hand and supporting the smooth implementation of the crisis plan. Here are two sample plans:

Sample Plan A:

1. Call 911.

2. Evacuate all students and staff.

3. Keep all people at a safe distance from building.

4. Have a designated person (usually the principal or assistant) to provide essential information to authorities.

5. Attempt to talk to the aggressor before the police arrive.

6. Do not try to disarm the aggressor by yourself.

Sample Plan B:

1. Call 911.

2. Using a code over the intercom (e.g., the teachers' room is closed), instruct teachers to keep all students in (preferably locked) classrooms and out of hallways.

3. Provide essential information to authorities.

4. Have a designated adult to attempt to talk to the aggressor.

5. Do not try to disarm the aggressor by yourself.

Ignorance is not bliss when it comes to needing a cooperative response when a crisis occurs in your school. Educating the entire school community is the first step to minimizing potential harm and avoiding potential violence before it develops. If everyone understands what to do and how to do it before a crisis erupts, they will follow steps that they have rehearsed.

Level 4 Intervention Form

Bringing a Weapon into School (with Intent of Using It)

(CONFIDENTIAL)

School: _____

Student's name: _____

Grade: _____ D.O.B.: _____/_____/_____

ID Number: _____

Dominant language: _____

Date: _____

1. Who Initiated Intervention?

_____ Student

_____ Other Student: _____

_____ Teacher: _____

_____ Other: _____

2. Description of weapon and circumstances surrounding its identification:

_____

_____

_____

_____

Initial Evaluation

I. Name: _____

Title: _____

Date of interview: _____ Report Attached: ___Yes ___No

II. Determined Concern of Risk:

_____ No Concern

_____ Minimal Concern

_____ Moderate Concern

_____ Major Concern

III. Explanation of Concern:

_____

_____

_____

IV. People and/or Agency Notified:

Name(s): _____ Date: _____

_____ Law Enforcement Notified: Name of Contact: _____

_____ Mental Health Agency: _____

Parental Meeting Scheduled for: Date: _____ Time: _____

Place: _____

V. Results of Meeting:

_____

_____

_____

Action Plan

I. Actions Taken:

_____ Student will be monitored over the next __ Week __ Month __ Other

_____ Student Suspended

_____ Student Expelled

_____ Student will receive support by:

  _____ (a) Meeting with Counselor

  _____ (b) Participate in Skills Classes

  _____ (c) Referral made to Agency: _____

  _____ (d) Peer Mediation

  _____ (e) Other: _____

II. Evaluation of Progress: Date of Observation: _____/_____/_____

_____ Noticeable attitude change

_____ Noticeable mood change

_____ Appearance

_____ Social interactions with peers

_____ Interactions with teachers

_____ Change in academic performance

_____ Other _____

Additional Evaluation of Progress:

_____

_____

_____

_____

III. Intervention Termination by: _____

Date of Termination: _____/_____/_____

Dealing with a Potentially Violent Student

If you are approached by a potentially violent student, it's important that you convey the correct attitude and message. Students with emotional problems will respond more readily to reasonable questions and demands of teachers who show common sense, authentic compassion, and a sense of neutrality. The following guidelines can help de-escalate a potential crisis:

1. **Be Aware**

   ◊ **Be aware of verbal cues.** Verbal cues communicate approximately 10 percent of our real message. By ignoring what an angry student is saying, you run the risk of escalating his or her angry feelings. Typical verbal cues may include abusive language, threats, or cursing.

   ◊ **Be aware of body language.** Body language (e.g., tenseness, clenched fists, staring into eyes, pointing fingers) communicates approximately 60 percent of your message.

   ◊ **Be aware of feeling tone.** Feeling tone communicates approximately 25 percent of your message. Loud volume, high pitch, and a fast rate of talking can be indicators of an angry student.

   ◊ **Be aware of self.** Being aware of your own communication can decrease the potential of a violent act.

2. **Respond—Don't React**

   Verbal:

   ◊ **Remain focused and in control.** Staying as calm and cool as possible but expressing concern in the face of a verbal challenge will help decrease a potentially explosive situation. For example, if the student raises his or her voice, lower yours. Speak in a conversational versus authoritative voice.

   ◊ **Listen and learn.** Listening to what a student is saying as well as validating feelings are powerful strategies for de-escalating aggression.

   ◊ **Calm feeling tone.** An angry student can become irrational fairly quickly, becoming unable to focus on actual words being communicated. He or she can "hear" your feeling tone, moderate volume of speech, and concern for his or her well-being.

Nonverbal:

◇ **Maintain appropriate distance.** Stand 2 to 3 feet or arm's length away from an angry student. Getting into a student's "face" will have negative results.

◇ **Maintain an open stance.** A non-threatening open stance with open hands in plain view will give a clear message of support and safety.

◇ **Maintain an empathetic facial expression.** Maintain eye contact without staring through the student. Your facial expression should be empathetic but not casual. Your expression should convey seriousness and concern.

Practice these safety techniques to increase your confidence and therefore the safety and success of your interventions.

Self-Help Activities

Following are activities for helping students feel comfortable talking about themselves or in a fun non-threatening manner.

1. **Ball-Toss Q&A:** You will need a beach ball or soft sponge ball that can be tossed among the class. Ask your students to sit in a circle or around the room so that everyone can easily catch the tossed ball. First ask the question, let your students think for a few seconds, and then toss the ball to a student. If they do not want to answer, they toss the ball back to you; otherwise they hold the ball until they are finished with their answer. The following sample questions can be used for different age groups:

- What makes you really happy?

- What really annoys you?

- What is one thing you like about where you live? One thing that concerns you?

- Who is the most interesting adult you know? Why?

- If you could change one thing about this school, what would it be and why?

- What do you think makes life difficult for kids growing up now?

- If you become a parent, how would you raise your children?

- If you were a teacher, what kind of teacher would you be? Why?

- What would be the best present you could receive right now? Why?

2. I Feel . . . Before starting this activity, ask students to suggest feeling words and write them on the chalkboard. Then ask students to complete the sentence "I Feel _____ when. . . ." They fill in the blank with a feeling word such as *frustrated, angry, sad, excited, okay,* or *scared.* After students complete the sentence, they can either toss the ball back to you or another classmate.

3. Word Associations. In this activity, you say a word and then toss the ball to a student who then says the first thought that comes to his or her mind (that is appropriate in school). Depending on the maturity of your class or student, hold a short follow-up discussion on any answer. Example words are:

- Stop
- Fight
- Resolve
- War
- Home
- School
- Peace
- Friends

- Enemy
- Learn
- Listen
- Music
- Help
- Love
- Hate

- Safety
- Crime
- Jail
- Free
- Education
- Control
- Responsible

4. Paper-Peer Feedback. This activity is done at the end of the week. Ask your students to sit in a circle and give each student three pieces of paper. Have students think of someone in the class that may have been helpful or kind to them during the week. Then think of someone who may have been annoying or mean to them during the week. Students then take turns walking over to the student and either giving him or her a piece of paper while describing the kind act or taking a piece of paper while describing the annoying behavior. The receiving student is not allowed to comment but instead must listen to the comment.

This activity not only can support positive classroom behaviors but can give your students a safe opportunity to express themselves in an assertive manner without having to be concerned about getting into an argument. It's surprising how honest students can be during this activity.

5. Group Beat. Ask your students to concentrate on listening to each other as well as to themselves during this activity. Have everyone close their eyes or look down at their table. Turn down the lights in the room. Then ask students to begin creating a simple beat with their hands by either clapping or slapping their desktops. At first there will be a lot of "noise," which will conflict in rhythm, but eventually something special will happen. The students will gradually begin to synchronize the sounds they are making into a pleasurable beat. Follow up this activity with a short discussion on what this activity has to do with school.

6. Burning Questions. Ask each student to write down a question he or she would like answered, then fold the paper and put it into a shoe box labeled "Burning Questions." Have a volunteer pick a question, read it to the class, and attempt to answer it. If the student needs help answering the question, he or she can ask a helper to assist in answering it. If the question cannot be answered, the student can put back it into the box and pick a new question. This activity can invoke a lot of humor as well as serious thought.

7. What's in a Name? Have students sit in a circle. Ask a volunteer (which may be you to start the activity) to offer the use of their name, and write it on the chalkboard. Moving around the circle, ask each student to make a word out of each letter of the student's name, describing the student. After everyone has contributed, the student whose name is on the board discusses the accuracy of the words chosen to describe him or her. For example:

J	O	H	N	H	A	L	L
O	R	E	A	E			
L	G	A	T	L			
L	A	L	U	P			
Y	N	T	R	F			
	I	H	A	U			
	Z	Y	L	L			
	E						
	D						

8. Carousel Opinions. This activity will help students explore personal opinions and beliefs about conflict. You'll need large sheets of newsprint, tape, and markers for this activity. Tape sheets of newsprint in four corners of the classroom. Write a different "conflict statement" on top of each sheet with a different-colored marker. Explain to your students that you want them to be able to share their opinions and that each sheet of newsprint has a statement written on top that reflects a view about conflict. Ask them to get into four groups and spend five minutes at each corner writing down a short statement about their opinion with the colored markers provided.

After all groups move around the room, ask students to discuss what they wrote and read by reviewing the statements written. Point out that listening to a classmate doesn't necessarily mean that you agree or disagree with him or her but is a sign of maturity and respect. You might write opinion statements like these:

- Conflict is never helpful.

- All people want to be liked.

- Schools promote kind acts.

- Drugs lead to violence.

- All conflicts can be solved.

- All guns should be banned.

- Sometimes you must hit back.

- Conflicts usually turn into violence.

- People are either violent or peaceful.

- Words can never really hurt you.

- Video games can lead to violence.

- Being bullied is part of growing up.

- Parents need to hit their kids sometimes.

9. The Communication Contract. Ask students to brainstorm a list of ideas that will help the class to work together by communicating effectively with respect for differences. To help them get started, write down a few agreements such as: "Talk one at a time," "Do not judge what someone is saying," "Wait your turn." After a discussion that includes questions such as, "Why is this suggestion important?" and "How would this improve the way we work together?" pass out the Communication Contract (p. 155) and ask students to write down the agreed-upon guidelines for working together. This sheet should be kept in their notebooks and referred to when needed. Post a large copy of the contract to remind all students of what they agree on.

Communication Contract

Date _____

To support positive communication and participation for the purpose of working together, I agree to follow and support the following guidelines:

1. _____

   _____

2. _____

   _____

3. _____

   _____

4. _____

   _____

5. _____

   _____

_____

Student signature

_____

Teacher signature

10. What Do You See? The purpose of this activity is to help each student gain a better understanding of how we all have our own points of view and that in every conflict there are sometimes several ways of seeing things. Explain that in order to solve conflicts, the people involved must be open to understanding different ways of looking at what caused the problem and possible solutions.

Ask your students to sit in a circle. Put a half-full glass of water on a table in the middle of the circle. Ask each student to look at the glass and decide whether it is half empty or half full. Take a tally of responses and explain that there is no right or wrong answer, just different perspectives. You can also share the theory that those who see the glass half full tend to be optimists. Next show the class a nicely wrapped box and ask your students to guess what's inside. After some discussion, reveal the mystery object and ask how they perceived what was in the box (e.g., the way it is wrapped, its size, etc.).

Distribute copies of the handout "What Do You See?" (p. 157) and ask students to describe what they see (two old men or a pretty vase). Explain that this handout also demonstrates the importance of understanding that we all see things from our own perspectives. Explain that because people often have different feelings, experiences, and understanding, they can see things in life differently. Ask the following questions:

- "How can two people get an understanding of each other's point of view?"

- "When trying to resolve a conflict, why is it important to understand another point of view?"

- "What makes it difficult to change your perception of things?"

11. Paired Interviews. Students who have anger problems or who may feel excluded from the mainstream school community need to make healthy connections with their peers. This will usually not happen unless an adult facilitates the initial connection. Use Paired Interviews to begin the process of building these positive peer relationships.

Write "Six-minute Interview" on the board as the agenda for this activity. Pair students by using random counting 1-2, 1-2, 1-2, and so on, or arrange the students yourself. Give each student a copy of the Paired Interview Form (p. 158) and ask them to decided which partner will begin the interview. Signal when six minutes has almost passed and then ask partners to switch roles.

After the interviews are completed, have students sit in a circle and introduce their partners to the class. Then have them share one or two things they learned about their partner.

What Do You See?

Directions: After looking at this picture, ask yourself the question, "What do I see?" There is no right or wrong answer to this question, but there are different ways of looking at the picture.

Name _____   Date _____

Paired Interview Form

Directions: These are questions you can use when interviewing your partner.
Write down your partner's answer to your questions.

1. What do you do after school? _____

_____

2. What is one thing you would like to change about this school? _____

_____

3. What's your favorite holiday and why? _____

_____

4. Describe your neighbor. _____

_____

5. What are you really good at doing? _____

_____

6. (Your Question) _____

_____

   (Your Partner's Answer) _____

_____

12. Fight, Flight, or Speak Up! This activity can help students develop alternatives for problem solving. You might introduce this activity by saying:

"Usually people are limited to two ways of dealing with conflict. One way is fighting, either with words, fists, or both. The other way is walking away from a conflict. We know fighting is a bad idea and walking away in some cases is the best and safest thing to do. But sometimes walking away doesn't work. Why not?"

Write their responses on the chalkboard.

"The third way of dealing with a conflict is to speak up or to be assertive by following these steps:

> *"1. Say what is bothering you without trying to hurt the other person's feelings or getting back at someone else.*

> *"2. In a firm voice, say what you'd like the other person to do differently.*

"For example: If someone calls you 'big head,' you could choose to get into a fight over this comment, walk away and ignore it, or speak up by simply saying, 'Leave me alone!' or 'I don't like being called names. So stop it!' Bullies don't expect their victims to speak up for themselves. If the bully continues calling you a name, then it's probably best to stay calm and walk away."

After giving an example, pass out the "Fight, Flight, or Speak Up!" activity sheet (pp. 160 and 161). While your students are filling out the activity sheet, walk around and check their responses to make sure the assertive statements are not aggressive or attacking the other person.

Fight, Flight, or Speak Up!

Directions: You are going to use your common sense to develop some new ways to handle conflict. Use the conflict problems to describe what the Fight, Flight (walk away) and Speak Up options might be. Read the example to help you understand how to complete this activity.

Example:

Conflict: You lend your friend a CD but when it's returned late, the CD is scratched and missing the box.

> *Responses:*
>
> • **Fight:** <u>Push your friend against a locker and threaten to hurt him if he doesn't pay for it.</u>
>
> • **Flight:** <u>Take the CD and say, "I guess I'll buy a new one."</u>
>
> • **Speak Up:** <u>This CD was in good condition when you borrowed it. I'd like you to buy me a new one without scratches and a missing box."</u>

Conflict: You're with some of your friends and one person begins making fun of another person who is not present.

> • **Fight:** _____
>
> • **Flight:** _____
>
> • **Speak Up:** _____
>
> _____

Conflict: A girl in your class accuses you of stealing something from her backpack. You didn't do it and have no idea who did.

> • **Fight:** _____
>
> • **Flight:** _____
>
> • **Speak Up:** _____
>
> _____

Fight, Flight, or Speak Up! (continued)

Conflict: You decide to pierce your ear. When you come to school, another student looks at you and says, "Hey Pete, don't you look pretty. I didn't know you were queer!"

- **Fight:** _____

- **Flight:** _____

- **Speak Up:** _____

_____

Conflict: You are on the school bus and someone comes up to you and says, "What are you looking at, retard?"

- **Fight:** _____

- **Flight:** _____

- **Speak Up:** _____

_____

Conflict: You're walking home and someone who is known to be a bully is riding his bike really fast toward you, turning just before hitting you. He stops and laughs at you.

- **Fight:** _____

- **Flight:** _____

- **Speak Up:** _____

_____

Bullying on the Bus

I live in a progressive rural community, a half-mile from our elementary school. It's a school many parents want their children to attend. My older daughter loved it and my two younger children also look forward to going to school every day. I work forty minutes away in an urban school district that has the best and worst of our public schools. The reasons for many of its challenges range from large class size, limited materials, and an overwhelming number of very needy children. It's not unusual to hear stories from these students about harassment on the school bus.

One day while talking to my children's elementary school principal, I mentioned how reassuring it is for a parent to not have to worry about unchecked harassment in our elementary school. She replied, "Yes, you're right. It all occurs on the school bus." It was surprising to hear that even in our progressive community, bullying and other undesirable behaviors are occurring where it can, on the school bus.

Millions of students ride school buses every day in this country. No one wants to have their school's anti-bullying policies end at the edge of the parking lot. In most cases the driver is the only adult on board. To transport students safely, the driver must watch the road, not the riders, during most of the trip.

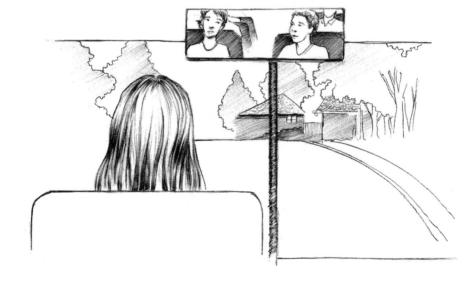

Of course, bus drivers have large mirrors and usually see fights, but they can easily miss harassing behaviors such as pushing, shoving, grabbing of clothing, and verbal abuse (which is typically sexual or racial). They can also miss comments about clothes, body size, or family income.

Students who are harassed on the bus, day in and day out, will most likely not want to participate in learning when they get off the bus. Some school districts hire adult monitors for buses, but most say this is too costly. Some have installed video cameras, often with a working microphone, hoping to deter would-be bullies and to help administrators determine who did what on the bus. Some school districts have proposed using parent volunteers aboard school buses; however, few districts use this option.

> **Key Concept**
>
> *Bullying can make the school bus experience a nightmare for targeted students.*

Here are some things you can do to make the bus ride safe for every student:

Conduct a School Survey: Find out if students are feeling safe on their buses. Ask questions that will determine the type of harassment and the degree to which it is or is not occurring.

Support Reporting: Create an atmosphere in which it is expected that not only the bus driver, but students, will report any incident on the buses. Create a team made up of students, drivers, teachers, parents, administrators and the manager of the bus company to develop a district plan for Respect and Responsibility on the Bus. List expected behaviors on the bus and make available behavior report forms to students in every classroom (see page 164).

Anti-bullying Pledge: Make it part of the district's *overt expectation* that before any student can ride a school bus they must sign an Anti-bullying Pledge. The student's parents are obligated to sign it as well as observers and supporters of respectful school bus behavior. See an example of a pledge on page 165.

Respect & Responsibility Bus Report

(CONFIDENTIAL)

Date: _____ Bus Number: _____ Time: _____

Student or Driver You Are Concerned About:

_____

What is the problem?

_____

_____

_____

_____

Your Name: _____

Grade: _____ Homeroom Teacher: _____

Names of anyone else who knows what happened:

_____

_____

_____

Thank You for Being Responsible.

Anti-bullying Pledge

The _____ School District's anti-bullying expectations apply to the school grounds and school buses. In order for you to ride on the school bus, you must read and sign this Anti-bullying Pledge agreeing to follow these expectations.

By Signing This Pledge, I Agree To:

- Treat everyone with respect.

- Help others in need.

- Follow all school and bus rules of behavior.

- Refuse to bully others.

- Refuse to watch or join in when someone is being bullied.

- Tell an adult.

Signed by Student: _____

Parent: _____

Increase Awareness: Bus drivers in school districts where bullying on the bus is addressed say that because bullying has been brought to everyone's attention, it's easier for them to stop it quickly by saying, "That is bullying behavior and not allowed on this bus or in school." A successful teacher, administrator, and parent has a goal to be constantly focusing on facilitating kindness, tolerance, and respect for one another. Schools can take on the task of creating awareness programs, which keep the issues of tolerance, respect, and kindness in the forefront of everyone's mind. One school brought in a trainer for the National Education Association's Bullying/Sexual Harassment Prevention/Intervention Program to conduct a training session for staff members. There are agencies throughout the country in many of our communities that can fill this role as well. During this awareness program, all teachers, administrators, students, parents and support personnel, such as bus drivers, custodians, and secretaries, can sign an Anti-bullying Pledge.

Anti-bullying Posters: These posters can be hung on the school walls and in school buses. All students and adults are recognized for their efforts in creating a culture of tolerance, respect, and kindness in their school buildings and on their buses.

Bystanders are Empowered: Bystanders can become part of the solution. When we empower others, we empower ourselves. Inclusive awareness programs can give hope to victims of bullying, whether in school or on the bus. As a colleague once shared, "They may have thought, 'This is going to be a long and difficult year at school'," she said. "Now they know there's a support system that encourages active participation to stop harassment, and that they don't have to put up with it. They know as we now know that bullying shouldn't and won't be tolerated."

Cyberbullying: The Invisible Risk

What Is Cyberbullying?

When "Jose," a ninth grader, checked his text messages, he found that he had to prepare for an after-school confrontation. The message read: "fight to finish—3:30 soccer field." When school let out that day, there was a crowd of students waiting to witness and cheer on a fight that had been brewing for days. Fortunately, a teacher overheard some students talking about it at lunch. This teacher showed up with a police officer. The crowd was dispersed, parents notified, and cell phones confiscated. For this reason as well as the fact that cell phones distract students from working and learning in the classroom, the Springfield, Massachusetts, School District recently voted not to allow student-owned cell phones to be used in school. Springfield, as well as many other school districts across the country, are realizing that cyberbullying may be impacting the school climate and consequently interfering with the ability of students to be successful in school.

Today's youth are actively using the Internet and cell phones as tools for interpersonal communication and socializing. They not only send e-mail but they create personal Web sites; post blogs (online interactive journals); send text messages; receive and send instant messages (IMs); talk in chat rooms; upload and share videos, or video network; and look for new friends on teen Web sites, such as My Space. IMing is a new way of communicating, and it's creating its own rules, grammar, and social protocols. It may feel like an easy way to chat, but students are actually creating a typed transcript that can be seen by anyone—without a delete button.

On the surface these social avenues may seem harmless and convenient, but in actuality they sometimes serve as tools for harassment or *cyberbullying*. The invisible risk of being bullied online is particularly tempting for students because anyone can disguise their identity and pretend to be someone else. For this reason many students will say or do things on a computer that they wouldn't dare say or do in person.

Cyberbullying can take different forms. Online fights are becoming more common in middle and secondary schools. Harassment in the form of sending mean messages can happen at all grade levels. Posting gossip or rumors to damage reputations is an anonymous way to divide a peer group. For example, one sixth-grade student posted a "top-five hated kids" list.

Cyber threats are often related to in-school bullying. The online bully can be the school bully. Sometimes the student who is victimized at school becomes an anonymous cyberbully and retaliates online.

Most cyberbullying that occurs takes the form of antisocial and mean-spirited behavior, such as:

- Repeated notes sent to someone's cell phone (text messages)

- Hurtful instant messaging (IM) conversations

- Threats sent via e-mail

- A Web site created to spread rumors and gossip or to damage someone's reputation

- Posting and forwarding unwanted pictures, videos, or private messages to others

- Using someone's screen name to post unwanted messages to everyone and anyone

When and Where Cyberbullying Takes Place

Students have little refuge from being a victim of cyberbullying. Because of the variety of avenues for communication, students are a target 24 hours per day. Cyberbullying can take place during school hours, in the library, at home, or virtually any place that a student is away from an adult and has access to the Internet or a cell phone. Adding to their own stress, many students who are targets of online harassment do not inform their parents, teachers, or any adult about being harassed.

Crystal, an eighth-grade student, was seen reading a text message after her Spanish class. She became visibly upset, and, when asked by her teacher what was wrong, she began to cry. Her teacher called for assistance so she and Crystal could have a private conversation. Eventually the student showed her teacher what she was crying about. A text message on her cell phone read, "You are a fat bitch who everyone hates." Crystal said that these disturbing text messages were becoming a frequent occurrence and that she did not know what to do.

Will was an outwardly happy student with two involved, caring parents who supported their children's use of computers from a very young age. As any concerned parent would do, they had discussions with their children about the dangers of the Internet. Periodic discussions with Will assured them that he was using the computer responsibly, and he was allowed to have a computer in the privacy of his bedroom. After Will's suicide, his father looked through Will's computer and found IM exchanges with another boy who was harassing Will in an extremely disturbing sexual manner. The messages demonstrated how these communications caused Will to change his view of life in a dramatically negative way, which led him to take his own life.

> **Key Concept**
>
> *Cyberbullying is sending or posting harmful material or harassing messages using the Internet or other electronic devices.*

No one knows for certain if this tragic death could have been avoided, but tragedies such as this one can give parents and teachers an understanding of the steps to take to help children avoid cyberbullying.

What Can Be Done

All of the major Internet service providers offer some form of parental and school controls. For example, AOL offers "AOL Guardian," which reports to parents on the Web sites their children have visited and who their children have exchanged messages with. Some schools are using a product called WebSense, which blocks most Web sites that may contain inappropriate content. Microsoft offers a similar product, *Content Advisor*, which prevents students from reading and seeing inappropriate content and lets adults set up an approved group of Web addresses. It also has a "restricted zone" of inappropriate sites.

However, these technological preventative measures can only do so much. Students in school as well as children in the privacy of their bedrooms eventually may find ways around some restrictive sites. For these reasons we need to establish clear rules, guidance, *and* monitoring, which will assist schools and parents with children's online adventures.

Helpful Steps for Schools

1. Schools must develop a clear, comprehensive policy for computer and cell phone use, both on and off school property. A description of what constitutes cyberbullying and a list of consequences should be included in the school's policy as well as a requirement to report all cyberbullying or threats by students and adults.

2. To prevent most of the obnoxious online material, school districts could implement a protective filter for each in-school computer.

3. Schools should require that all students who are using the computers either in a computer lab, the classroom, or on portable laptops, read and sign the "Cyberbullying Awareness Contract" (see p. 173).

4. Teachers and other staff members must be mindful of the public nature of their online activities. Guidelines for electronic communication with students and parents should be part of the teachers' job.

Helpful Steps for Parents and Teachers

1. Teachers and parents must effectively monitor and respond to cyberbullying that takes the form of "harmful speech" or they run the risk that they will eventually have to respond to school violence or to a student suicide attempt.

2. Students should use computers in open spaces where they can be seen. It's a good idea to set time limits for use at home and in school.

3. Here is an important message to communicate to students: "Don't make threats online. If you are found to make a cyber threat, even if it's meant as a joke, you could be suspended or even arrested."

4. Talk about what is and is not appropriate while working or socializing online. Educate students on how harmful online speech and behavior can violate criminal laws, which include: making threats of violence to others, making obscene or harassing phone calls (e.g., text messaging), perpetrating hate crimes or sexual exploitation, or using a cell phone to photograph someone in a place of expected privacy (such as a bathroom or locker room).

5. If there is *reasonable* suspicion that a student is engaging in cyberbullying behavior, school administrators can conduct an individual search of computer and Internet use records.

6. Parents need to understand how to use a computer and understand what can be seen online. They have the right to monitor and check their child's computer use any time with or without prior warning.

7. Develop strategies for student bystanders to encourage them to identify and report cyberbullying behavior.

Helpful Steps for Students

1. **Don't give out personal information.** This includes real names, pictures, e-mail addresses, or anything that can identify you to people you met on the Internet. *Remember: It's not uncommon for kids to be sexually exploited online!*

2. **Don't share passwords.** Parents should be given your password for safety checks, but do not share passwords with friends, who may share them with people who will use the passwords for negative purposes.

3. **Delete unwanted messages.** These include messages from people you don't know or who seem mean and unsafe.

4. **Understand the Internet.** There is no privacy. Others can easily copy, read, or print what you say or see pictures you send.

5. **Report unwanted messages.** It is your responsibility to protect yourself and others by telling a trusted adult when you receive unwanted online messages.

Cyberbullying Awareness Contract

School's Name: _____

Student's Name: _____ **Grade:** ____

Date: _____

As an educational institution, which has a responsibility for the welfare of all of our students, it is important that we do everything we can to make sure you understand the rules and guidelines for using the Internet in school and at home. In order to receive permission to use a computer while at school, you must read and sign the following contract. A copy will be kept at school and another given to you and your parents. Thank you.

I Will Not:

⬦ Post any information online that could be insulting or harmful to others.

⬦ Exchange pictures or give out e-mail addresses to people I may meet on the Internet.

⬦ Retaliate to cyberbullying messages by returning hurtful or threatening messages. (**Never reply to harassing messages.**)

⬦ Give out private information, passwords, names, addresses, and so on that can be used by online bullies to hurt me or someone else.

I Will:

⬦ **Report cyberbullying toward me or a peer to a trusted adult.**

_____   _____
Student's signature   **Teacher's signature**

Resources

Additional Reading

Bullying at School by Dan Olweus (Cambridge, MA: Blackwell, 1993). This leading psychologist gives good advice on how to stop bullying in schools.

Childhood Bullying and Teasing by Dorothea M. Ross, Ph.D. (Alexandria, VA: American Counseling Association, 1996). A good review of literature and strategies that can be used by school counselors and others.

Group Exercises for Enhancing Social Skills & Self-Esteem Vol. I & II by SiriNam S. Khalsa. (Sarasota, FL: Professional Resource Press, 1997 & 1999). "This book(s) is a must for any professional who works with groups in a variety of settings," Jack Canfield.

How to Talk So Kids Will Listen and Listen So Kids Will Talk by Adele Faber and Elaine Mazlish (New York: Avon Books, 1991). These authors are students of Giam Ginott. This book is filled with illustrations on how to talk and listen to kids of all ages and in all situations.

Inclusive Classroom, 2nd ed., by SiriNam S. Khalsa (Tuscon, AZ: Good Year Books, 2005). I wrote this book as a practical guide for all educators who teach in a multi-level classroom. This book covers learning styles, teacher teamwork, adapting work, managing behaviors, working with parents, and differentiated instruction.

The Morning Meeting Book by Roxann Kriete (Greenfield, MA: Northeast Foundation For Children, 2002). This is a comprehensive and user-friendly guidebook for K–8 teachers on how they can implement Morning Meeting in their own classrooms.

Odd Girl Out: The Hidden Culture of Aggression in Girls by Rachel Simmons (Orlando, FL: Harcourt, 2002) describes three types of aggressive behavior in girl bullies.

100 Ways to Enhance Self-Concept in the Classroom by Jack Canfield and Harold Wells (Needham Heights, MA: Allyn and Bacon, 1993). The authors of the "Chicken Soup for the Soul" series wrote this easy-to-implement book of activities to help educators support positive self-esteem in all students.

Reducing School Violence through Conflict Resolution by David W. Johnson and Roger T. Johnson (Alexandria, VA: Association for Supervision and Curriculum Development, 1995). This book addresses how schools can create a cooperative school environment where students learn peer mediation and conflict resolution skills.

Teaching Discipline and Self-respect by SiriNam S. Khalsa (Thousand Oaks, CA: Corwin Press, 2007). This book includes effective strategies, anecdotes, and lessons for successful classroom management taken from my 25 years of teaching experience. "SiriNam has offered solutions to our country's schooling problems that are realistic, optimistic and full of promise," Jeffrey Ryan, Ph.D., Massachusetts Teacher of the Year 2003.

What to Do When Kids Are Mean to Your Child by Elin McCoy (Pleasantville, NY: The Readers Digest Association, 1997). This practical book helps parents of children ages 5–13 effectively deal with bullying, rejection, and fear of others in school.

Books for Kids

Bullies Are a Pain in the Brain by Trevor Romain (Minneapolis: Free Spirit Publishing, 1997). I like the balance of humor and seriousness in which this author addresses bullying. It offers practical advice for children ages 8–13.

Bully on the Bus by Carl W. Bosch (Seattle: Parenting Press, 1988). The main character is being bullied on the bus. The author asks the reader to help decide how he should handle the situation. For grades 2–6.

Cliques, Phonies, & Other Baloney by Treavor Romain (Minneapolis: Free Spirit Publishing, 1998). This author discusses why cliques exist and how to feel good about yourself. For grades 3–8.

Everyone Is Good for Something by Beatrice Schenk de Regniers (New York: Clarion Books, 1980). This book addresses self-esteem and self-confidence. Everyone tells the Boy he's good for nothing until he rescues a wise cat and helps save some lives. For grades 3–8.

How to Handle Bullies, Teasers and Other Meanies by Kate Cohen-Posey (Highland City, FL: Rainbow Books, 1995). Dealing with prejudice can be a consistent problem for adolescents. This book addresses this issue as well as bullying and teasing. For grades 6–10.

Loudmouth George and the New Neighbors by Nancy Carlson (Minneapolis: Carolrhoda Books, 1988). This fun book deals with prejudice and friendship by making the analogy with a family of "dirty" pigs who move next door and George wants nothing to do with them until his friend starts to spend time with them. For grades 2–6.

Loudmouth George and the Sixth-Grade Bully by Nancy Carlson (Minneapolis: Carolrhoda Books, 2003). The author deals with bullying walking to and from school in a light manner that can lead to serious discussion. For grades 2–6.

Say Something by Peggy Moss (Gardiner, ME: Tilbury House, 2004). In this book an upper elementary student learns the importance of responding when she observes students on her bus being bullied or left out. For grades 5–8.

Why Is Everybody Always Picking on Me? A Guide to Handling Bullies by T. Webster-Doyle (Middlebury, VT: Atrium Society, 1991). This book has stories and activities that can help students resolve conflicts in a peaceful manner. For grades K–5.

Organizations

Center for the Prevention of Hate Violence

University of Southern Maine
207-780-4756
www.preventinghate.org

The Center conducts training programs to help schools develop civil and respectful climates. Students, professionals, parents, and bus drivers can learn intervention strategies to stop degrading language.

Center for the Prevention of School Violence

20 Enterprise Street, Suite 2
Raleigh, NC 27607-7375
1-800-299-6054

This organization helps support safe schools through newsletters, research bulletins, and articles to keep professionals and parents informed.

Educators for Social Responsibility (ESR)

Cambridge, MA 02138

1-800-370-2515

www.esrnational.org

ESR helps students develop the commitment to create a safe and responsible world community. Their Web site includes additional activities for teachers and students.

National Institute for Urban School Improvement, Education Development Center, Inc.

55 Chapel Street

Newton, MA 02458-1060

617-618-2189

www.inclusiveschools.org

This Center disseminates information packets, posters, and other material that promotes inclusion in our urban schools across the country.

Teaching Tolerance

400 Washington Avenue

Montgomery, AL 36104

334-956-8374

This organization is a national education project dedicated to promoting respect and understanding in our classrooms. They offer an excellent magazine, *Teaching Tolerance*, as well as posters and other material at no cost to teachers.

Internet Safety Organizations

Center for Safe and Responsible Internet Use

474 W. 29th Avenue

Eugene, OR 97405

541-556-1145

http://new.csriu.org/

The Center for Safe and Responsible Internet Use offers research and outreach services for safe and responsible use of the Internet. One of the books they offer is *Cyber-Safe Kids, Cyber-Savvy Teens* by Nancy E. Willard.

Media Awareness Network

1500 Merivale Road, 3rd floor

Ottawa, Ontario, Canada K2E 6Z5

613-224-7721

Toll Free: 1-800-896-3342 (in Canada)

http://www.media-awareness.ca

MNet educates children and parents on the effective use of media. The Parents section of the site offers tips for talking to children about media and advice on managing media use at home.

Teenangels

http://www.teenangels.org/

A division of WiredSafety.org, this group of 13- to 18-year-old volunteers has been trained by law enforcement officials in aspects of online safety, privacy, and security. They educate schools and communities on how to be safe on the Internet.

Wired Safety

http://www.wiredsafety.org/

This Web site helps victims of cyber abuse as well as parents with issues, such as children using MySpace and YouTube.